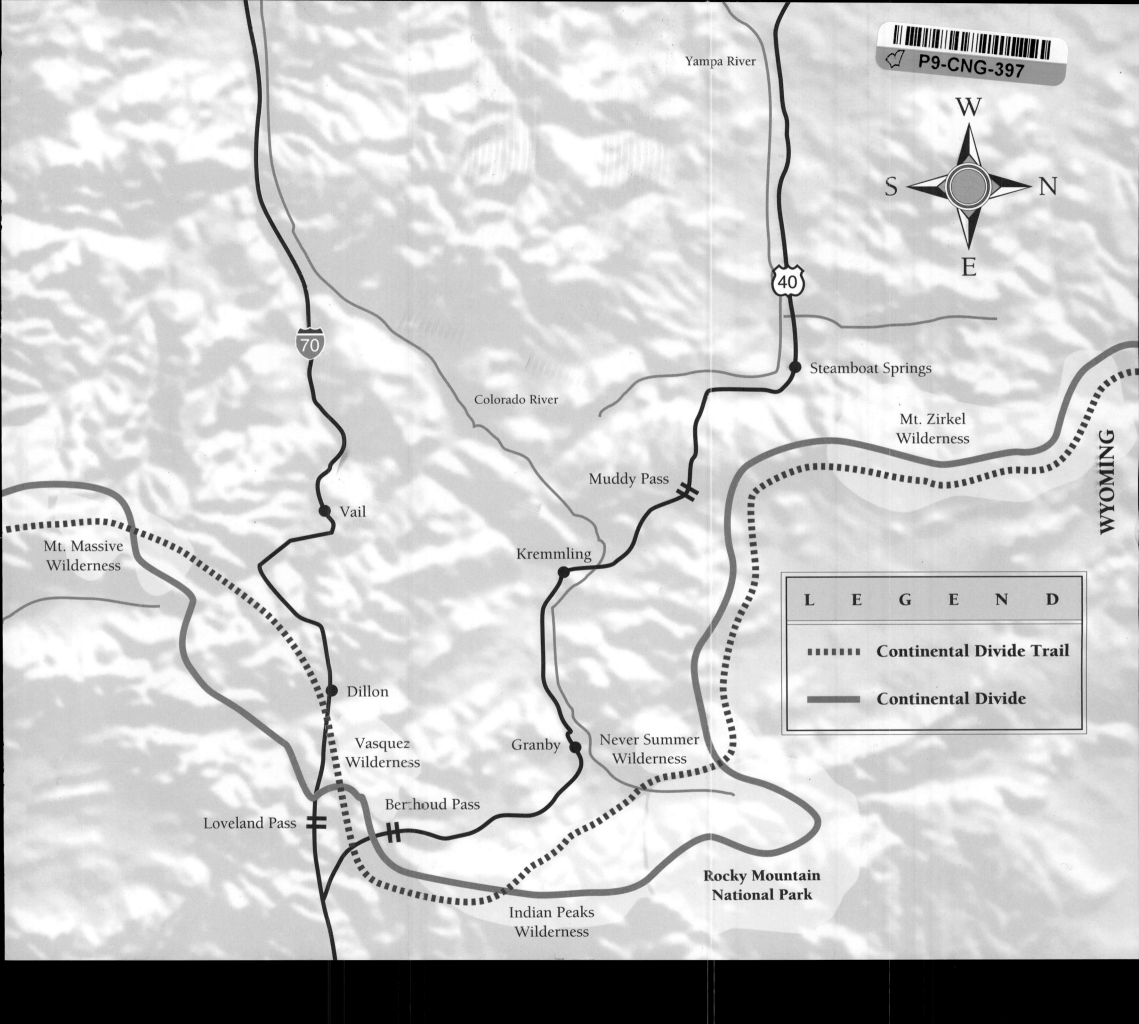

Yampa River

P9-CNG-397

W
S ⊕ N
E

40

Steamboat Springs

Mt. Zirkel
Wilderness

Colorado River

Muddy Pass

WYOMING

Vail

70

Mt. Massive
Wilderness

Kremmling

LEGEND

▪▪▪▪▪▪▪ Continental Divide Trail

━━━ Continental Divide

Dillon

Vasquez
Wilderness

Granby

Never Summer
Wilderness

Berthoud Pass

Loveland Pass

Rocky Mountain
National Park

Indian Peaks
Wilderness

MOUNT ANTERO (14,269') REFLECTS ON A TARN, SAWATCH RANGE

Sunset in the South San Juan Wilderness

Along
Colorado's
Continental Divide Trail

PHOTOGRAPHY BY JOHN FIELDER

TRAIL STORIES BY M. JOHN FAYHEE

WESTCLIFFE PUBLISHERS

ENGLEWOOD, COLORADO

PUBLISHED BY WESTCLIFFE PUBLISHERS, INC.
2650 SOUTH ZUNI STREET
ENGLEWOOD, COLORADO 80110

PRINTED IN HONG KONG BY C & C OFFSET PRINTING CO., LTD.

PRODUCTION MANAGER: HARLENE FINN

EDITORS: TOM LORANG JONES & CATHERINE OHALA

DESIGN: MARK MULVANY

PRODUCTION: TIM GEORGE

INTERNATIONAL STANDARD BOOK NUMBER: 1-56579-227-0

LIBRARY OF CONGRESS CATALOGING-IN-PUBLICATION DATA

Fielder, John.
    Along Colorado's Continental Divide Trail / photography by John
Fielder ; text by M. John Fayhee.
        p. cm.
    ISBM 1-56579-227-0 (alk. paper)
    1. Continental Divide National Scenic Trail—Pictorial works.
    2. Hiking—Continental Divide National Scenic Trail. I. Fayhee, M.
John, 1955- . II. Title.
GV191.42.C86F54 1997
917.88—dc21   97-5916
                                                        CIP

OTHER JOHN FIELDER BOOKS IN PRINT

Photographing the Landscape: The Art of Seeing
Rocky Mountain National Park: A 100 Year Perspective (with T.A. Barron)
Explore Colorado, A Naturalist's Notebook (with the Denver Museum of Natural History)
Cooking with Colorado's Greatest Chefs (with Lynn Booth)
A Colorado Autumn
A Colorado Kind of Christmas (with Laura Dirks and Sally Daniel)
To Walk in Wilderness (with T. A. Barron)
Colorado, Rivers of the Rockies
Along the Colorado Trail (with M. John Fayhee)
Colorado, Lost Places and Forgotten Words

Colorado Littlebooks:
    Wildflowers of Colorado
    Colorado Waterfalls
    Colorado Reflections

TO ORDER TITLES OR TO RECEIVE A FREE COLOR CATALOG, CALL WESTCLIFFE PUBLISHERS AT 303-935-0900
OR FAX 303-935-0903.

ACKNOWLEDGEMENTS

I wish to thank two summer's worth of "sherpa" helpers for carrying gear on the trail, cooking, camp setting, fishing for protein, assisting in the photography, and being good friends. They are my son JT Fielder, Jon Osborne, Dave Nessia, Byron Jones, Jamie Feinstein, Mike Hayse, Joel Smiley, Dave Sanders, and Brett Mill. Thanks to Tommie, Tensing, and for the most part, Kerwood, for being such good llamas. Pogo, you are officially retired! Thanks also to Evan Cantor for his wonderful illustrations that appear throughout the book. Evan is a nature artist, writer, and musician from Boulder whose perception of the natural environment makes this a better book. *This book is dedicated to my Uncle Fred, who brought me to Colorado.*

JOHN FIELDER

The process of taking two months off work and hiking 700-plus miles through the middle of nowhere is not easily achieved by one's lonesome. I had a lot of help both during the hike and during the process of putting this book together. As far as gear procurement is concerned, I would like to thank the good folks at Wilderness Sports in Silverthorne, Colorado; Gregory packs; Fabiano/Scarpa boots; Katadyn water filters; and Crazy Creek camp chairs. On the food-drop-assistance front, I would like to thank Chuck Gangel (my father-in-law); Currie Craven; Mark Fox; Patrick Brower; and Aurel Burtis. A big thanks to the Powers That Be at Wolf Creek Ski Area for letting me park my car in their lot for a week, as well as to the owners of the Western Belle Motel in Lake City, Colorado, for seeing to it that I got a ride back to the trail. I would also like to thank my bosses, Bob Brown and Michael Kirschbaum of Eagle-Summit Newspapers, for allowing me to take a two-month leave of absence. Kudos, too, to Tom Jones, friend, co-worker and editor of this tome, for keeping his wits while dealing with all those wild verb-tense changes for which I am infamous. And, of course, many thanks to John Fielder, picture-taker extraordinaire, for giving me the opportunity to write this book in the first place. It was fun. Last, hugs and kisses to my wife, Gay Gangel-Fayhee, for revolving her life around yet another of my trips. *This book is dedicated to Joseph Brown Dischinger, my dearest and most long-lived amigo, without whose help and support I never would have moved to this wonderful place called Colorado.*

M. JOHN FAYHEE

Part of the proceeds from the sales of this book benefits the Continental Divide Trail Alliance

Colorado Guidebooks:
    Colorado's Continental Divide Trail: The Official Guide (with Tom Jones)
    The Colorado Trail: The Official Guide (with Randy Jacobs)
    The Complete Guide to Colorado's Wilderness Areas (with Mark Pearson)
    Colorado's Canyon Country: A Guide to Hiking & Floating BLM Wildlands (with Mark Pearson)
Annual Colorado Calendars:
    Colorado Scenic Wall Calendar
    Colorado Scenic Engagement Calendar
    Colorado Wildflowers Wall Calendar
    Colorado Reflections Wall Calendar
    Colorado Parks & Monuments Wall Calendar
Other:
    Colorado Writing Journal
    Colorado Scenic Address Book
    Colorado Note, Christmas, and Postcards

ALONG THE TRAIL NEAR UTE CREEK, WEMINUCHE WILDERNESS

ALONG THE TRAIL, MOUNT ZIRKEL WILDERNESS

FOREWORD

John Fielder

It was the end of May and things did not look promising for any of us. After two years of planning, it appeared that nature's capriciousness would delay each of our journeys by most of a summer. And most of a summer meant that two books would be published a full year late.

I will not soon forget the flurry of phone calls between John Fayhee, Tom Jones, and myself as the summer of 1995 was about to begin. The winter of 1994–95 had deposited plenty of snow, and the spring had been as cold and dreary as any I'd seen in my 25 years in Colorado. The oldtimers could not remember a deeper snowpack in Colorado's high country in the past 50 years. And only as summer was about to begin did the snow start to melt.

This was the summer that the three of us, each on separate expeditions, had planned to hike the almost 800 miles of the Continental Divide National Scenic Trail (CDNST) through Colorado. John Fayhee was to write anecdotally about his experiences for a sequel to our 1992 book, *Along the Colorado Trail*; Tom Jones would document the route for a guidebook; and I was to photograph for both. Now we all had visions of snowshoeing for most of the 800 miles, and I was imagining two books filled with white photographs!

The majority of Colorado's Continental Divide Trail (CDT — same trail, slightly different name) is at or above treeline (almost 12,000 feet). Of its entire length, some 3,100 miles from Mexico to Canada, our portion has the highest average elevation by far. Even if we had the hottest June on record, we knew that hiking during the prime months of July and August was in jeopardy. As it happened, June remained cold and snowy in Colorado's high country, and by mid-June we knew that July would be lost. Tom and John made reconnaissance forays into the backcountry, I made a couple of overflights, and by the beginning of July we made the decision to extend the project into 1996.

During the most unusual year of meteorology I have ever seen in Colorado, in the summer of 1995 aspen trees leafed at the end of June — a full month late (and never even turned to gold that fall), alpine snowpacks were up to 12 feet deep as July began, most alpine lakes were still under snow and ice, and the wildflower bloom peaked in the middle of August instead of July. No part of Colorado was better off than any other, though the San Juans did melt off sooner than other mountain ranges. As a result, Tom Jones and I spent August and September hiking portions of the CDT. John Fayhee's trek and journal required that he experience not only the entire trail, but that he suffer the accomplishment — and resulting sublime thoughts that accrue from pain and agony — in one fell swoop, 62 days to be exact.

The year 1996 was more normal meteorologically. We only had to contend with the usual adversities: heat, cold, wind, rain, snow, and exhaustion. By September of 1996, Tom Jones had hiked the entire trail, John Fayhee had averaged 14 miles per day in one continuous trip, and I had pieced together the CDT in a way that allowed me to photograph each major segment when it was at its most beautiful. I had hiked parts of the trail before, so I was able to be at the right place at the right time for rephotographing (which always yields entirely new work) wildflowers, mountains, waterfalls, and lakes along this highest stretch of America's rooftop.

To be sure, Colorado's CDT courses high country. Most of my memories are of infinite views in all directions obscured only by mountain peaks and low-lying storm clouds. It is a world without end, a place most comfortable for those who normally are ill at ease with man made walls and windowless rooms. Nevertheless, the designers of the trail allow hikers to experience more than just the alpine ecosystem. Much of the spine of the Continental Divide is precipitous and rocky, and not hikeable. For this reason, and to let hikers experience lush forests of spruce and fir, half of the CDT is not on high. My most memorable times on the trail occurred breaking out of the trees onto the tundra and retreating during thunderstorms to the shelter of sweet-smelling forests.

As you enjoy my images made during two summers on Colorado's CDT, as well as John Fayhee's stories of life on the trail, it might be helpful to remember the logistics of our separate hikes. John stayed on the trail the entire way and his accounts reflect that. I wandered on and off the trail in an attempt to photograph the Continental Divide itself, not only what one sees from the trail. For the most part the CDT remains near the Divide. However, in some places, such as in Summit County and Rocky Mountain National Park, many miles separate the two. John and I did not walk together, nor did we even meet once along the way. (Tom Jones and I met by accident on Rollins Pass. Was he glad to have lunch inside our shuttle vehicle during a thunderstorm!) I used llamas most of the time to carry gear, while John carried food and gear exclusively on his back. Most of the trail photos depicted herein are of me and my group of sherpas and llamas, though photographs of John made by his wife, Gay, appear from time to time. John hiked the trail from south to north, probably the best direction if you are hiking the entire CDNST from Mexico to Canada, but inconsequential for just the Colorado portion. Snowpacks do not seem to melt any faster in the San Juans than they do in the Zirkels.

This book will acquaint you with the spine of the Colorado Rockies. I hope it will tempt you to hike Colorado's CDT in its entirety or just portions of it. If so, I suggest that you consult a copy of *Colorado's Continental Divide Trail: The Official Guide* by Tom Jones. (Guides for the balance of the CDNST from Mexico to Canada published by Westcliffe Publishers are forthcoming.) Whether you hike the CDT or not, may these views and words engender within you a greater appreciation for all things wild and natural.

Englewood, Colorado

The Continental Divide, Rocky Mountain National Park

INTRODUCTION

M. John Fayhee

i thank You God for most this amazing
day: for the leaping greenly spirits of trees
and a blue true dream of sky; and for everything
which is natural which is infinite which is yes
— e.e. cummings, from *XAIPE*

I was living in Silver City, New Mexico, in 1980 when word came out of the nearby Gila National Forest office that a new long-distance footpath had been legislatively established by an act of Congress. It was to be called the Continental Divide National Scenic Trail, and it was basically supposed to follow the Divide all the way from Antelope Wells, New Mexico — located on the Mexican border — to the Canadian border at Glacier National Park, Montana. Having just finished hiking the entire 2,100-mile Appalachian Trail the summer before, I was, to say the least, intrigued by the notion of a mountain time zone equivalent of the famed AT.

Several Forest Service employees skewered my enthusiasm by telling me that, just because Congress legislatively "created" a hiking trail didn't mean it would ever exist on the ground. I was cautioned to not hold my breath waiting for the CDT to become a physical reality. The year 2000 was tossed around as the earliest the 3,100-mile trail might actually be completed. To a be-here-now-type 24-year-old backpacking junkie in 1979, that was too far in the future to even ponder.

The very next fall, though, I met a group of four hikers who were less than a week away from completing this trail that was supposedly at least 20 years away from existence. They had left Glacier National Park while the snow was still hip deep and, after averaging almost 30 miles per day, were bearing down fast on the Mexican border. I lassoed these four hikers, dragged them out to a local watering hole, plied them with cheap alcohol and made them tell me everything there was to know about the CDT.

The first thing they told me was that there really wasn't a "real" trail connecting Canada with Mexico. There was, however, a basic conceptual route that was strung together throughout the '70s by a man named Jim Wolf, who had undertaken the task of proving that it was possible to build the CDT.

The four hikers I met in Silver City told me they had had to follow a dizzying combination of trails, dirt roads, paved roads and open country in order to complete their trek. When I met them, they were hiking entirely on dirt roads.

I decided right then and there that, one day, the CDT and I would become chums, but I did not want to hike it until it was a little better defined. A couple years later, I moved to Colorado and thoughts of the CDT faded to my mental back burner. In the meantime, I honed my long-distance, high-alpine hiking skills by completing the 500-mile Colorado Trail in 1991. Three years later, I started hearing about the CDT again.

When Congress legislatively established the CDT, it sort of neglected to allocate any cash for the planning and construction of the trail. As the four hikers I met in New Mexico indicated, it wasn't even close to existing as a unified trail. The U.S. Forest Service was flagged by Congress as the agency responsible for seeing to it that the CDT got built, but the Forest Service had to do so utilizing its status quo budget and resources. This bad fiscal situation was exacerbated by the fact that, within the Forest Service itself, there was no person or committee charged with coordinating CDT planning and trail-building efforts. It was left to individual ranger districts to build or not build the trail. And this does not even factor in National Park Service, Bureau of Land Management and private lands. In short, the CDT would have been an organizational mess, had there been any organization to mess up.

Thus, for 16 years, the CDT languished. It was a nice idea whose time had not yet come. But pretty much out of the blue, in 1994, the National Forest Foundation, a non-profit group established by Congress to help the Forest Service fund capital improvement projects, designated the CDT a "high priority." The Forest Foundation told the Forest Service it wanted to raise $3 million for the CDT. The Forest Service jumped into action so fast it tripped all over itself.

The National Forest Foundation's efforts marked the beginning of some heavy-duty CDT momentum that has gained strength during the last several years and shows no signs of letting up. The Foundation spawned the Continental Divide Trail Alliance to oversee future fund-raising for trail building and maintenance of the entire 3,100 miles from Mexico to Canada, and to promote its use. By 1995, the CDT through Colorado was de facto done, predominantly using existing trails and dirt roads. Though it was very far from completely buffed and marked, it was very possible to hike from the Colorado/New Mexico border near Cumbres Pass to the Colorado/Wyoming border near the Encampment River.

In 1996, I decided to do just that, and this book is the story of my 740-mile, nine-week hike along the Colorado section of the CDT. I hope you enjoy the book as much as I enjoyed the hike.

I have an apology to make before we get going, though: While English is richer than any other language, there are only so many synonyms for a lot of the words I had to use frequently out of image-setting necessity. I practically wore my Thesaurus out looking for adjectival alternatives — but there are limited synonyms of "beautiful," "splendid" and "awe-inspiring." (And this in a state that can use up all the scene-based superlatives the language can muster.) That makes for some verbal redundancy. Ditto for "steep," "precipitous" and "lost." You'll just have to get used to those words and their few linguistic cousins. Please forgive me, but soon you will understand.

Breckenridge, Colorado

I

CUMBRES PASS TO WOLF CREEK PASS

The South San Juan Wilderness

In a retrospect borne of many blisters and a whole lot of map-and-compass-based head scratching, it seems only appropriate that the defining incident of my two-month, 740-mile hike from New Mexico to Wyoming along the Colorado section of the Continental Divide National Scenic Trail occurred before I had even started the trek.

My hiking partner, Gary Michaels; my wife, Gay; my dog, Cali and I had arrived at Cumbres Pass (located a few miles north of the New Mexico border), where we would begin our hike, in the middle of a torrential downpour at about 5 p.m. on Saturday, July 13, 1996. While Gary and Gay were perfectly content to wait the storm out in the van, I was antsy after the six-hour drive from our home in Breckenridge.

I donned rain gear and enthusiastically egressed the van. After three years of planning, I was so eager to get going, I would have been happy to hoist my pack and start hiking to Wyoming right then and there. Gary and Gay, on the other hand, were disposed to wait until morning. As I stood there, Gore-Tex clad in the heart of this wonderful High Country thunderstorm, I was trying desperately to clear my mind in anticipation of my upcoming adventure. As is the case with most of my long trips, I had been working frenetically up until the very last minute getting my domestic and vocational ducks in a huddle before hitting the trail. Thus, I was tense to the point of near numbness from all the frenzied pre-hike preparation. Moreover, like most 40-year-old Americans these days, a lot of civilization-based detritus has taken up more or less permanent residence in my cranial mainframe and, since the next morning I was set to embark on this gnarly Divide Trail excursion, I wanted very badly to jettison as much of that excess mental baggage as I could before taking my first steps. In martial arts, we call this "emptying your cup" — the idea being that, before you can be receptive to and embrace the new, you have to get rid of as much of the old as possible.

As soon as I was out of the van, I saw what I immediately assumed to be the Divide Trail traversing a hill a hundred or so yards away on the other side of a skunkweed-infested meadow. I said to myself, "Well, Brother Fayhee, there she is — the trail that will be the center of your life for the next nine weeks." But, as the rain rattled my Gore-Tex like a snare drum symphony, my confidence that I was eyeballing the right trail started to ebb. While I was trying to concentrate

meditatively on cleansing dark thoughts of mortgage and car payments being unmet and the two publications I edit going out of business while I was tromping through the woods all summer, the notion that maybe the trail I was looking at on the other side of that meadow was not the CDT began to germinate, gestate and dominate my contemplation.

I mean — I knew on an intellectual level that the trail before me had to be the CDT. After all, I was near Cumbres Pass, which the CDT crosses, and, to the best of my knowledge, there are no other trails in this vicinity. But, for some reason I couldn't yet grasp, my heart started sending directional red-alert messages to my brain, and I have been lost enough times that I always, always pay close attention to such messages. An overt fear of messing up right out of the chute was washing up on the beachhead of long-lived anal retentiveness and paranoia.

This fear might be silly, but it is not totally unfounded, as the CDT has the reputation of being often ridiculously under-marked. And, since the CDT goes all the way from Mexico to Canada, I was starting in the middle, not at the beginning. Thus, there were no signs or plaques or billboards or flashing neon lights at this spot. My mental cup started to fill to brimming with nightmarish notions of happily hitting the trail in front of me the next morning, only to find out some hours later that I was not on the CDT heading toward Wyoming, but, rather, on some long-abandoned stock driveway meandering toward Sonora.

Now, you may ask, why didn't I just pull out the fine set of hyper-detailed topo maps I surely had in my possession? Well, to be honest, my map situation for the six-day, 62-mile stretch from Cumbres to Wolf Creek Pass would have earned some well-deserved scowls from even a low-ranking Boy Scout. We had but two non-topographical maps — one 1:120,000-scale 1975 Rio Grande National Forest map and one 1992 San Juan National Forest map of the same scale — between us. They both had the CDT marked on them, but my pre-trip itinerary-planning marathon revealed that the trail upon the maps and the trail upon the ground were decidedly different animals. And nowhere, I had been forewarned, was this reality more poignant than in the vicinity of Cumbres Pass.

Psychologically, I cannot abide the concept of getting lost before I even begin the hike. That's something that would, somehow, instantaneously get back to every single one of my hiking

ALONG THE TRAIL, HEADWATERS OF THE NAVAJO RIVER, SOUTH SAN JUAN WILDERNESS

AUTUMN IN NAVAJO RIVER COUNTRY

SOUTH SAN JUAN MOUNTAINS

JON OSBORNE FISHING FOR BREAKFAST

buddies, all of whom would take particular delight for the next three decades in recounting at every opportunity how Fayhee, the self-professed man of the mountains, got lost on the Divide Trail before he ever got onto the Divide Trail. I would have to change my name and move to a Buddhist monastery in Bhutan.

In reality, my map situation was neither as flippant nor as slack as I make it sound. Bill and Mary Kay Stoehr, the owners of Evergreen, Colorado-based Trails Illustrated, had graciously supplied me with maps covering the entire Divide Trail route through Colorado. But, at that time, they had yet to come out with a map for the South San Juans. For the rest of the hike, I was well mapped. It was just for this section that I was sort of naked on the map front — which wouldn't have made me feel any less idiotic had I become hopelessly lost between here and Wolf Creek Pass. The thing is, even the most recent 7.5-minute quads offered by the U.S. Geological Survey are way out-of-date when it comes to the CDT.

As the rain finally started to abate, Gary and Gay slowly and groggily emerged from the van. I decided to investigate the trail situation in detail. But, of course, I had to act cool and on top of things. The last thing I wanted at this point was for Gay and Gary to know I wasn't sure we were in the right place. After all, I was the leader of this adventure and I would have hated for their confidence in my leadership to wane before it had a chance to wax. I make some glib comment about wanting to stretch my legs and start angling my way over toward that now-suspect, unfortunately signless trail. It took 45 minutes before I was convinced that, though directional befuddlement surely awaited me somewhere on this hike, it would at least not happen immediately. I ended up walking about a half mile north on the trail — which, in that distance, offered up no indication of its identity or lineage — before turning around

and nonchalantly moseying back in the direction of camp, whistling a tune with my hands in my pockets, like I didn't have a care in the world.

The tread petered out as it made its way through the woods a scant 100 feet from the van. At last, I caught sight of an old, sap-filled blaze on a spruce and, 15 minutes later, at a point near where this thus far rather unimpressive excuse for a National Scenic Trail crossed the highway, almost under a dilapidated railroad trestle, I found a faded and broken sign that let me know, sure enough, I had been beating feet along the world-famous CDT.

I lightheartedly walked back to camp, Cali as ever within a few feet of me having the time of her life. Gary and Gay had the tents set up, so there was little left for me to do but return to my pondering spot to try once again to clear my mind. Unfortunately, the exact opposite started to happen. The fact that I had just spent almost an hour trying to ascertain if the trail before me was the correct one weighed somewhat heavily on my mind. "Is this the way this hike will be?" I asked myself, somewhat fretfully, my cup overflowing right before my eyes.

More than that, though, I realized that I was stressing out big time about the fact that I was the self-professed, self-ordained leader of the Great NM/WY/CDT Expedition. I was the one who set the whole thing up and planned the itinerary. Gary had done absolutely nothing in the way of planning and, at this point, couldn't have found his way to Wyoming if his life depended on it. I had assumed the role of group captain, and Gary was perfectly willing to follow the leader. And Gay always leaves trip planning and logistics to me. Success on this trip was on my back and I was feeling ready to explode from tension as a result. In all my previous long hiking trips, it has just been me at the beginning of the trail. Whatever

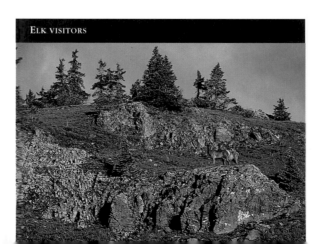

ELK VISITORS

screwups I made affected me and me alone. This go-round, many things would be different.

We had agreed reveille was to sound at 5:15 a.m., with our initial departure set for 7:00. I did not sleep well that night. We were close enough to the highway that passing cars kept me from slipping easily into the Land of Nod. Plus, Cali was staked outside on a leash at the head of the tent. She fidgeted all night. I believe I have the only dog on earth who is afraid of the dark. Gay, who will be hiking with us only as far as Wolf Creek Pass, and I both suspect she would sleep uninterrupted through the night — allowing us to do the same — if we let her into the tent. But, I was resolute

MOSQUITO DEFENSE

that no hound of mine was ever going to become a wussy tent dog. There are people I know who would look askance at me if they learned I let my cur snooze inside my tent. My wife, on the other hand, would invite the dog in, turn down her bed, stick a mint under her pillow and read her a bedtime story. So, sure, being a card-carrying husband and all, I knew beyond the shadow of a reasonable doubt that, eventually, I would succumb to the woeful, doe-eyed stares that both my wife and my dog boast in spades and let Cali into the tent. But I was bound and determined that such an indignity would not transpire on the very first night out.

Our plan of attack the first day was to hike 12.2 miles to Dipping Lakes. But, because of my map's lack of topographical features, I had no earthly idea that the first eight of those miles were decidedly uphill in nature — all the way to the

SUMMER ALONG THE NAVAJO RIVER

12,200-foot summit of Flat Mountain. Eight straight miles of uphill is tough under any circumstances, much less on the first day of a nine-week hike.

We had all tried very hard to make our packs as light as possible for this stretch, so as not to expire before we even had the chance to work up a good case of tendonitis. We weighed our packs before we left Breckenridge. Gary's was 46 pounds; Gay's, 38 pounds; Cali's, 11; mine, 50.

The first few miles passed through light and airy woods punctuated by numerous babbling brooks. The birds were tweeting and, even though we were all fairly constantly aware of the fact that our packs felt like someone had stuffed them full of lead, it was great to finally be on the trail. I actually had a bounce in my stride that lasted almost until noon, when most every body part south of my clavicles started hurting at the same time.

Less than an hour from Cumbres Pass, we encountered our first wildlife — a porcupine. When we first talked about bringing Cali on the hike, the subject of porkies permeated our discussions. I have had other dogs that have made physical contact with porcupines, so I know from experience that there are whole truck-loads of negative ramifications to be had on the needle-to-mutt front. We had purchased from our local vet enough in the way of tranquilizers and painkillers to sedate and make happy a rhino, much less our 55-pound cur. (It is no fun at all to try pulling porcupine quills from the snout of a wide-awake dog who's in excruciating pain.) I also bought a Leatherman tool, which has a set of serrated pliers that could be used to rip quills from any of the most likely anatomical resting places of quills — the gums, face and chest. This was a nightmare we hoped with all our hearts to avoid.

Cali is a very obedient trail dog, so, even though she saw the porkie as it made its way up a tree, when I called her, she immediately returned to my side. Since she never strays far and since she never harasses wildlife, I only leash her when we pass other people on the trail.

We stopped for our first lunch in a thick pine forest. For almost every lunch and snack during the entire hike, I planned to eat nothing save Gay's homemade granola bars — which are like neutron stars of nutrition and calories. Though I love them dearly, I could manage to eat only half a bar, saving the other half for later. By the end of this hike, when my body fat is down below five percent, I will be snarfing down as many as four of these bars a day — at about 750 calories a pop. (Don't try this at home, kids.)

Shortly after lunch, we entered a small meadow, where we encountered a herd of about 30 mad cows. Having lived in New Mexico for five years, I know what it's like passing cows on the trail. The main thing I know is that they are unpredictable, to say nothing of large, creatures. Some herds of cows just stand there, watching you pass, with the dumbest looks of any animal on the planet. Some herds will run for their lives when hikers approach, as though they "think" we are looking to put our freeze-dried A-1 Steak Sauce to good use right then and

SOUTH SAN JUAN MOUNTAINS

AUTUMN IN THE SOUTH SAN JUAN MOUNTAINS

CHALK MOUNTAINS, SAN JUAN NATIONAL FOREST

DIPPING LAKE

there. Others will stand their ground and snort. I have been chased through the woods on numerous occasions by cows with some sort of bug up their rectum.

These cows, though, did nothing but tip their hats to us; but, when they laid eyes on Cali, their dander got up. They chased her from one side of the meadow to the other, and back again. They were out for doggie blood, and Cali thought it was the most fun she had had in several days. I finally had to put my corpus delecti between the dog and the killer cows, so she could effect a safe escape and so we could stop laughing long enough to commence walking again.

After three hours of ascending, we finally entered the Krummholz Zone — the bionomic area that serves as a buffer between the forest and the tundra. With the views opening up to the west, we were, less than half a day from Cumbres, in the mountain lover's equivalent of Shangri-la. I cannot believe this area isn't the most popular part of the state, yet we have seen nary a soul. In every direction, as far as the eye could see (and the eye could see very, very far), there were waterfalls and meadows and streams and flowers and colorful cliff faces and dark blue lakes.

I was happy as a pig in slop and I could scarcely keep from giggling. I was mirthful not only because of the scenery, but, at the same time, it was finally starting to sink in that I was finally on the trail, pointed north toward Wyoming. Of course, Wyoming was not exactly close, but that was a Good Thing. It had been five years since I began a long hike and I was looking forward to it on all levels. I was curious to see how my increasingly decrepit body would handle the heart and soul of America's longest and hardest hiking trail. I was

ON THE TRAIL AT BLUE LAKE

delirious at the thought of snuggling against the bosom of Nature at her best for 62 straight days. And, well, I was delighted at the thought of being away from work for nine weeks.

More than anything, though, I was giddy about how much time I would be spending above treeline. There is nowhere I would rather be than in the alpine tundra, and, from what I had heard, the South San Juans boasted more in the way of above-treeline territory than any other part of Colorado, and that is saying a mouthful.

Just before topping out on Flat Mountain, we spied a monstrous herd of elk. We got within a half mile before they spotted us and ran, dissipating like a brown cloud over a ridge and out of view.

By now, we were walking for two minutes, then stopping for two minutes to catch our breath. The long uphill haul, the steepness of the terrain, our heavy packs, our out-of-shape legs and the altitude were combining to work their fatigue magic. Gay and I live at 9,600 feet, and Gary had spent a month in the High Country acclimating for the hike. But, even so, once you start getting over 12,000 feet, huffing and puffing and slow walking become the norm.

Once we topped out, we entered the South San Juan Wilderness, a 158,790-acre piece of alpine heaven on earth. Though there was no overt contrast between the wilderness and non-wilderness at this point, I felt the change that comes over every aficionado of untamed Nature when he or she enters an official wilderness area. It's like coming up for air in a world gone mad. It's like the ultimate sigh of relief. It's like freedom, however temporary and perhaps false, from the ever-present and oppressive tumult of things like work and mortgage payments.

So far, the trail had been of fairly good quality and easy to follow. Route-finding Grim Reality set in once we passed Flat Mountain. We were now in grassy tundra dotted with numerous small lakes, known as glacial tarns, even though it has been an exceedingly dry year in this part of the state. The suddenly treadless route was now marked with rock cairns

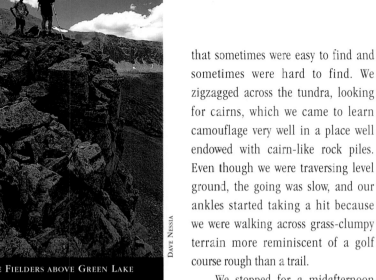

DAVE NESSIA

THE FIELDERS ABOVE GREEN LAKE

that sometimes were easy to find and sometimes were hard to find. We zigzagged across the tundra, looking for cairns, which we came to learn camouflage very well in a place well endowed with cairn-like rock piles. Even though we were traversing level ground, the going was slow, and our ankles started taking a hit because we were walking across grass-clumpy terrain more reminiscent of a golf course rough than a trail.

We stopped for a midafternoon snack next to a small lake. We were all running out of steam. Cali took a swim and I soaked my feet. I was wearing a pair of Fabiano Trionics, my all-time favorite hiking boots, but they had been recently resoled and, thus, were not riding like they used to. I was already getting a heel blister, and one of my little toes was banging pretty badly. In anticipation of possible boot problems, I had stashed a new pair of Vasque Clarions in our car. But that was still 53 miles and five days away at Wolf Creek Pass. I ate 20 or 30 Advils and hoped against hope that I was not going to be dealing with sore feet for the next 700-plus miles. I've hobbled down that path before and it's no fun.

Just after hoisting our packs, we saw our friends, Tom Jones and Tom Jones, Jr., hiking our way. It was their van we had driven to Cumbres Pass. They had started hiking south from Wolf Creek Pass seven days prior and we knew we would be passing them our first or second day out. I yelled out something borderline obscene about their obvious lack of manliness, then walked up to them — realizing too late that I had just insulted two men who were not the Joneses at all, just a couple of innocent hikers making their way blissfully across the tundra. Extracting my foot from the depths of my gullet, I sheepishly apologized for my lack of decorum and we talked trail skinny for a few minutes. The two men agreed that the route to Wolf Creek was very hard to follow and they told us to expect to get lost at least several times a day.

Great.

After two more miles of cairn-chasing (at one point, I had to drop my pack and wander around for 10 minutes to

find the trail), we began our descent back into the trees and down into Dipping Lakes.

I was fairly beat, but Gay, Gary and Cali looked like they were about to expire. Even before setting our tent up, Gay and I went down to the lake to wash up and change clothes. If there is one ritual I adhere to at the end of every hiking day, this is it. To call what I do "bathing" is probably too grandiose a description. First of all, this procedure is done sans soap, because even brands that market themselves as "biodegradable" are still funky from an environmental perspective, as they do not break down as quickly as the manufacturers would have you believe. Also, since I am the biggest cold water weenie in the history of the world, I rarely go any deeper than my knees. From that point, I dunk my washcloth, scrub down, count my goosebumps and leave the frigid water as fast as possible.

Ordinarily, if there's a body of water within 10 miles, Cali will enthusiastically seek it out and, unenticed, jump in and start swimming laps. The fact that I had to coax her into the water by repeatedly throwing a stick a few yards from shore spoke volumes about how exhausted my canine was.

After washing up and filling our water bag, we returned to what ended up being a very nice little campsite. It was, unfortunately, also mosquito infested. I would rather deal with any type of negativity than mosquitos. If the Terminator cruised into camp in a really foul mood, that would be better than mosquitos. I grew up in the fetid swamps of Tidewater, Virginia, and left that part of the country about 11 seconds after graduating from high school mainly because of mosquitos. Yet, at the same time, I hate using mosquito repellent, which, if it's a brand that works, is a poison's poison and, if it's one of those perfume-smelling natural brands, doesn't work. So, I lit up a monster stogie and began playing like a chimney. It was, as a means of vexing the mosquito hordes, an exercise in futility, as well as a fast track to dizziness. Still, it's fun to hear them coughing as they achieve attack formation, and I like knowing that I'm helping them all develop lung cancer.

Shortly after dinner, the little flying bloodsucking scum drove us into our tents, which was a good excuse to hit the sack at 7:00. I staked Cali out in front of the tent again, and, just before zipping the bug netting closed, I noticed there were at least 100 mosquitos on her snout and several dozen on her ears. She looked beyond miserable. I felt those woeful, doe-eyed stares burning a hole in my resolve. If it had been anything else besides mosquitos, I swear I would never have let her into the tent. But, let her in I did, and she spent the next hour wagging her tail so hard it sounded like the side of the tent was getting whopped by a grizzly bear's paw. Gay and the hound winked at each other, and my bride turned down Cali's bed, stuck a mint under her pillow and read her a bedtime story. Both Gay and Cali were conked out in about 0.2 nanoseconds.

I, on the other hand, was laying there awake pondering in a little more detail that unfortunate grizzly bear thought I just stupidly had. The South San Juan

GREEN LAKE

POND, SOUTH SAN JUAN WILDERNESS

Wilderness' reputation is based primarily upon the fact that many people say grizzlies still live here. Though there are many more people who say they don't, if they did, this would be the only part of Colorado with a grizzly population. They once roamed this state in great numbers, but grizzlies are considered by the Colorado Division of Wildlife to be extinct in Colorado, much to the embarrassment of many of us who hate having to deal with the superior smirks of people from Washington, Montana, Idaho and Wyoming when the subject gets around to which state is the toughest and the baddest.

John Fielder has talked to ranchers who are firmly convinced there are grizzlies hereabouts. And, every year or two, some scientific expedition enters the South San Juans with an eye toward answering the grizzly question once and for all. But, everyone knows that, if one of those expeditions ever found a grizzly or evidence of a grizzly, they would never even consider releasing any information, for fear of indirectly causing grief for the bear(s) in the form of hordes of curious animal lovers, over-zealous biologists and/or local ranchers who don't like the idea of a protected, monstrous, carnivorous endangered species dwelling in the same vicinity as their cattle and sheep. So, the fact all these researcher-types say there are no grizzlies in the South San Juans does not necessarily mean there are no grizzlies in the South San Juans.

Nine-tenths of me hopes very badly that there are still grizzlies here. The other tenth — though wishing earnest health and long life to every grizzly left on the planet and all — would prefer, if there are grizzlies in the South San Juans, they be located very far from my tent. Like maybe in Nevada. I once undertook a long and remote off-trail hike in Glacier National Park the same summer three people were killed there by grizzlies. I don't believe I slept a wink in 10 days. I was scared to death constantly. It was then that I realized I am phobic of large carnivores. I resolved to avoid camping in grizzly territory after that.

Better for the bears; better for me.

There is talk about re-introducing grizzlies into the South San Juans, a concept I support unconditionally and absolutely. But, if such a re-introduction ever takes place, my days of hiking in these parts are over.

Better for the bears; better for me.

Even if there aren't grizzlies in this neighborhood, there certainly are black bears. I have talked with several people who have seen black bears in the South San Juan Wilderness. I have never been as careful about bear-proofing my camp as I should. Technically, you should not cook close to your tent, you should not sleep in the same clothes you cooked in, and under no circumstances should you keep food or anything that has contacted food in or near your tent.

BLUE LAKE

ALONG THE TRAIL, SOUTH SAN JUAN WILDERNESS

MIDDLE FORK OF THE CONEJOS RIVER, SOUTH SAN JUAN WILDERNESS

Well, I pretty much blow off all three of those things most of the time, and toss and turn from dusk till dawn as a result, fully expecting, any light now (probably tonight) to wake up with a bear knocking on the front door of my tent. I have heard that having a dog in camp serves as a bear deterrent. For all I know, though, Cali could be a four-legged, mobile package of bear bait.

One of the best things about the Colorado High Country is that it gets cool enough at night that mosquitos have to hunker down. It's rare for the first mosquito to lift off before 8 a.m. So, we enjoyed our bowls of instant oatmeal, at least as much as anyone can enjoy a bowl of instant oatmeal, under mosquito-free skies.

Again, we were on the trail early. Today would take us 11 miles to Blue Lake, another place I don't know from Adam, except that I have seen it on a map. Ten minutes from camp, Gary realized he had forgotten his sunglasses. Gay went ahead on very good tread, while I waited in a pine grove between the two Dipping Lakes. I did not yet trust Gary's ability to find his way unguided. Presumptuous of me, perhaps, but smart. Best not to get separated until we have a feel for each other.

We are soon again above treeline, and, every few minutes, we pass more elk. Sometimes, they are in small same-gender groups. Other times, there are dozens of them. This time, we see numerous huge bulls and many cows with calves. It is a scene serene in a way that only the tundra in full bloom and full summer luxuriance can be.

We wound around the side of a small ridge that marked our first elbow-rubbing with the Continental Divide since Cumbres. We would be either directly on or within sight of the Divide for the next 200 miles. The trail stayed pretty much on grade for an hour, allowing us to hike in a relaxed manner, while still making good time. The tread, which had been well defined since Dipping Lakes, changed at Trail Lake (which should have been named Trail Ends Here Lake or Lack of Trail Lake). We found ourselves, once again, cairn-hunting while walking on those ankle-killing clumps of tundra grass. We crossed a small pass and descended onto an amazing lake-dotted, 12,000-foot-high treeless plain that was Vermont-like verdant. We stopped next to a small tarn for water and so I could soak my feet, which were getting worse fast. The blister on my right heel was so big and raw it looked like a bloodshot eyeball staring up at me. My little toe looked like it had been grabbed and twisted by a set of pliers held by a weight lifter experiencing an epileptic seizure. I also had a perplexing, yet impressive, array of mini-blisters on the inside heels of both feet.

Time to turn on the Zen hiker's trance that every long-distance backpacker knows so well. When we got back on the trail, I worked hard to separate a mind striving to be tranquil from a set of feet that felt like there were shish kebab skewers sticking in them like voodoo doll pins. Sometimes this works, sometimes it does not.

CASE'S FITWEED, SOUTH SAN JUAN WILDERNESS

WATERFALL, SOUTH SAN JUAN WILDERNESS

We were once again back on good trail and by midafternoon we switchbacked into the trees and a wide, dry valley. We hadn't seen a trail marker in several hours, and the directional demon was starting to visit me again. At the bottom, we intersected another trail where there was finally a sign with an arrow to BLUE LAKE pointing up and an arrow to GREEN LAKE pointing down. Justifiably ignoring this inane sign, we noticed there was one trail going straight ahead and one going to the left. No up or down trails that we could see. Maybe the local Forest Service trail crew was trying to be metaphorical. Maybe they were telling us that Blue Lake is Heaven and Green Lake is Hell. Either way, since our map really wasn't helping us out at that particular moment, we flipped a coin and took the trail to the left (perhaps this one goes to Purgatory), but it quickly petered out (which seemed only appropriate for a trail to Purgatory). I have never understood how good-quality trails can just suddenly end in the middle of nowhere. It's sometimes like there's a herd of lunatic trail erasers running through the woods. It was obvious that people have gone through here, though, because there were snippets of social trail and occasional hoof and boot prints in the dirt. Just as my direction paranoia was starting to reach fever pitch, the trail quality inexplicably improved. So, we were now hiking on good trail, but it still could have been a good wrong trail. Gary and Gay started getting nervous, too, so at a small creek crossing I asked them to take their packs off and make themselves comfortable. I, likewise, de-packed and headed off to see if I could learn where we were and where we were going. If we were on the right trail, we should have been within two miles of Blue Lake.

That guess ended up being about right. I made it to the lake and back in an hour. We all shouldered our packs and finished the day's walk, which, for me, was now 15 miles instead of 11. I kept waiting for Gary to say something like, "Hey, good job. Next time it'll be my turn to scout ahead." He didn't even broach the subject.

Blue Lake, it turned out, was, if not heaven, then at least heavenly. Framed by small cliffs on the far side, it was tucked into the heart of a dense coniferous forest. Clouds were moving in fast and we could hear thunder off in the distance. So, we bathed quickly and prepared to batten down the hatches. When the storm hit, we were all snug in our tents. There are few things more pleasant than taking a snooze in a tent during a rainstorm after a long day on the trail.

Snooze I did.

The storm moved in and moved out several times, so, during one break in the clouds, I jumped out of the tent to start fixing dinner, a provocative dehydrated bean-and-beef concoction with the last of our skanky cheese and moldy tortillas. Once again, we were in mosquito country, to the degree that we were all slapping ourselves so frequently and so hard while we tried to eat that anyone walking past would have thought he had just stumbled onto a group of highly motivated hambone enthusiasts.

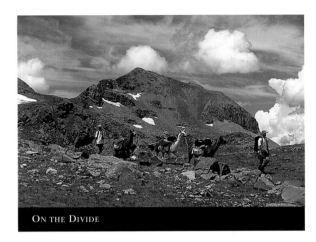

ON THE DIVIDE

Once again, the mosquitos gave us a good excuse to hit the sack early, which was good, as the next day we were facing what looked to be our first hard day — 13 miles to the Adams Fork of the Conejos River.

By the time we reached the Lake Anne Trail intersection at 11 a.m., we had made only four miles. We stopped for lunch in the middle of a herd of at least 2,000 sheep. Cali boasts very little in the way of identifiable pedigree, but there is little doubt she has some Australian Shepherd blood coursing through her mongrel veins. She was so excited we had to tie her to a tree. She had no idea what she wanted to do with all these sheep, but she wanted to do it very badly. Had I thought there was any chance I could have trained her in the next two minutes to herd these foul wool-bearers into the next county, I would have done so in a skinny minute. I don't know which I hate more in the wilderness, herds of cattle or herds of sheep. I guess it's a tie.

It took three miles of hard hiking before the stench of sheep urine faded from our nostrils.

After an hour of steep climbing, the overgrown and poorly defined trail immediately drops into the Middle Fork of the Conejos. The scenery is splendid and wild, but there are few things more irksome to a long-distance hiker than

FALLS, SOUTH SAN JUAN WILDERNESS

almost instantly losing the 2,000 feet he or she just gained.

During this toe-cruncher of a descent, my feet felt like they were being put through a meat grinder. I winced with every step; I winced at the thought of every step. Before we left Blue Lake, I had applied to my feet several dozen acres of Mole Skin, Mole Foam, tape, bandages and Band Aids. The problem was, there simply was not much in the way of non-blistered skin left on which to attach all those things. I had blisters on top of, under and immediately adjacent to blisters. My blisters were fighting battles with each other for territorial rights. The monster eye-shaped wound on my right heel now looked like the orb the Cyclops sported in Jason and the Argonauts. And then there was my poor tootsie, which had already lost its toenail, as well as several inches of length. I now had an ingrown toe.

I would never have guessed that the simple process of getting one's boots resoled could wreak such bad-fit-oriented havoc. I had had these boots for four years and hiked hundreds and hundreds of miles in them with not so much as a hot spot. And they are still in great shape. But, now, instead of old friends joining me on one last hike, they were torturous demons bent on making my life miserable. At the same time, my custom-made orthotics seemed to be collapsing, explaining the discouraging friction situation on the insides of my heels. After all my pre-trip preparations, I couldn't believe this was happening. Between boots and orthotics, I had $650 on my feet, yet I would probably feel better hiking barefoot across a bed of nails.

We stopped for a snack at the Middle Fork and I made mention of my foot problems for the first time, telling Gay and Gary that there was a very good chance I would not be able to hike any further today. I decided to soak my feet for a few minutes in the lovely, ice-cold cascading creek. Some of the Moleskin gets yanked off — taking skin with it — as I remove my socks. I believe I might have let a few bad words slip out along about this time. But, after soaking my feet and eating a tantalizing mixture of Advil, Nuprin, Aleve and aspirin ("pain gorp,"

PICKING UP THE REAR

I call this mixture), I felt much better and we started heading up toward a gorgeous pass just as a rainstorm hit. This marks the first time we had to hike in rain gear, and it's one of those scenes where it rains, we stop, take our packs off, put our Gore-Tex on, put our packs back on, hike 12 steps, rain stops, sun breaks out, we stop, take our rain gear off, hike six steps, rain starts again.

By this point, we were looking for a place to camp. We were all beat, and, even though my feet were merely

JON OSBORNE AND JT FIELDER ABOVE BLUE LAKE

excruciatingly painful — which is quite an improvement — I didn't want to push my luck. The problem was, we hiked and hiked above treeline along the side of the Divide looking for a place that was within a half mile of water that had a slope of less than 45 degrees. There simply was no such place. When we arrive at a saddle above the Adams Fork, I can tell Gay is whipped. But the closest water is 1,000 feet below and, since the trail pretty much parallels the creek as it descends, several miles away.

It is a long, hot and dry descent. I spend most of the time coaxing Gay and offering words of encouragement. I have never learned over the years whether she likes or appreciates me doing this during times of on-trail fatigue and woe, but one thing is clear: she expects it, as well she should. It's like, with every cajoling syllable, every exhortation, I am verbally paying penance for putting her in such an uncomfortable situation, when we could be sitting on a beach in Mexico.

Finally, I run ahead to look for a campsite. That way, when Gay gets there, I can just help her off with her pack, give her a hug, tenderly tell her what a stud she is and point her to a good sitting log. I reflect as I dash ahead that, before she met me 13 years ago, Gay had never backpacked — never even considered backpacking. Though she has developed an overall taste for it, she'd probably be a lot more comfortable right now if she'd hooked up with someone as devoted to, say, antique-hunting as I am to schlepping a pack up and down mountains all day. But, she made her choice and, as a result, she now has several thousand backpacking miles under her belt. She still doesn't really like carrying a pack (I mean, who does?), but she loves accessing the backcountry, especially when that backcountry is located in her native state.

The first piece of flat ground I came to was a grassy meadow backed up to a stand of pines next to the creek with great views in all directions. Ten minutes after I picked out a tent site, Gay and Gary arrived. They were mightily impressed with the digs. We all agreed it was definitely worth the effort to get here. And we made it to our predetermined goal for the day, which titillated the group leader part of my psyche.

The process of putting together an itinerary for a hike of this duration is complex and tedious, while being, under the best of circumstances, the very definition of an inexact science. This was especially so with the Divide Trail. It took me about a week to plan my entire 147-day Appalachian Trail itinerary in 1979 and about two days to plan my 43-day Colorado Trail trek in 1991. That's because those trails are literally guidebooked to tenth-of-a-mile increments.

At the time of my CDT hike, such was far from the case with regard to this trail. While the two volumes of Jim Wolf's Divide Trail guidebook series that cover Colorado certainly proved very helpful during the itinerary-planning process, they were only partially accurate, as the trail no longer follows Wolf's route in many places. Thus, I had to use a combination of Wolf's books, Trails Illustrated maps, national forest maps of varying scales and ages, and, when applicable, Colorado Trail maps. There were times when I had four sets of maps spread out on my kitchen table, and all four of those maps were in disagreement as to where the trail went. (The definitive series of CDT guide books, published by Westcliffe Publishers, is only now hitting book stores — too bad!)

While it was fun in a hair-pulling, jigsaw puzzle-solving sort of way, it was nonetheless exasperating, and it took more than a month of fairly steady effort.

ALONG THE TRAIL, SOUTH SAN JUAN WILDERNESS

But, still, detailed planning for a long hike is absolutely necessary. When planning a 62-day jaunt through the heart of the Rockies, you have to do more than simply say before the hike, "I will take so many days to make it between these two food-drop points." Often, once you're out in the woods, that's what it ends up being, but I have always found that scheduling each day out along the entire route prior to departure is the best way to go. This is not to say that I stick with that detailed itinerary come hell, high water or mangled feet. But, having a goal for each and every day serves as both a motivating tool and an easy-to-digest gauge of progress made. As well, except in the case of the most egregious planning foul-ups, you know there will be water at the place you choose as a campsite while sitting at your map-covered kitchen table half a year before ever leaving on the hike. As a matter of fact, water is usually the sole consideration when putting a detailed, day-to-day hiking itinerary together. Most times, it's better to have water in a place that ends up being less than perfect aesthetically than to dry camp in a pretty spot.

Success on a long hike is defined in many ways; but, first and foremost, it's defined by finishing the hike, and that is best achieved by winning a series of small victories along the way. Today, we celebrated a small victory. We made it 13 miles, Gay was still my wife and my feet were still mostly attached to my legs.

While Gay and I were down at the creek bathing, we hear some high-decibeled foul language emanating from camp. Upon returning, we learned that Gary's brand-spanking-new tent tore while he was setting it up. The wound was not severe, but, since he bought the tent only a week before leaving on the hike, Gary was justifiably miffed.

While he was executing a foul-mooded field repair, I started inventorying my food stash. It seemed like I had over-erred on the side of caution with regards to rations, so I donated several pounds worth of instant oatmeal and dried beans to the local raccoon population. That's always an iffy choice from the wilderness survival perspective, and one that merits some well-deserved scorn in the environmental community, but it was a decision that earned the earnest thanks of my back.

As the sun set, some wonderful alpenglow colored the high cliffs of the Divide to the south. There were very few mosquitos, so we could hang out comfortably outside, smoking and watching the sun set over this astounding locale. We had not seen anyone all day and it looked like we were the first people in a long time to camp at this spot. I don't know why that makes a campsite feel better and more special, but it surely does.

Again, I did not sleep well. I tossed and turned, worrying about my life back in Breckenridge. I even had several work-related dreams — a very bad sign of civilization-based mental pollution. I could not believe how I had let the stress of modern life infect my inner being like this.

The next morning, we passed through the last and the best part of the South San Juan Wilderness. We hiked all morning at 12,200-plus feet, along a plateau that spread in every direction for miles beneath Summit Peak, Montezuma Peak and Long Trek Mountain. I had heard stories about this magnificent place, but had always figured they were a little tainted by embellishment and exaggeration. But, both the facts and the spirit of those tales were true. With storm clouds gathering and the full power of the Colorado tundra welling up around us and within us, we exited the wilderness area. I am a man who has trod atop some tundra in his time, but never before had I experienced alpine grandeur of this degree and caliber.

Two miles later, we arrived at Elwood Pass, which ended up being the antithesis of our Adams Fork campsite. It proved that you can't always guess right when you're planning a long hike. We had to dip our water cup by cup from a mud-filled spring while it deluged. And our tent sites were lumpy and angled. But, as I relaxed under a fir as the dusk gathered, it felt like this modest expedition had some momentum going. And, for the first time since we left Cumbres Pass, my mental cup started to feel empty. I still could not say beyond the shadow of a reasonable doubt that the trail ahead would not dismay and perplex me to the point of anger and discouragement a million times; but, in this moment, such thoughts do not seem to matter. A lot of my heretofore near-bouts debilitating civilization-based detritus was dissipating into the chilly, soggy air, right alongside my cigar smoke.

Finally.

Two days later, we strolled out at midday at Wolf Creek Pass amid hordes of Winnebago-driving tourists taking pictures of each other in front of the Continental Divide sign next to the parking lot. We never did pass the Joneses, and that had me a little concerned; but, aside from a little cairn-hunting, we had not gotten lost once. And we were feeling strong.

I walked 20 minutes down the highway to Wolf Creek Ski Area to get Gay's car, and an hour later we had hotel rooms in Pagosa Springs, where we planned to take a day off.

Then, it was time to jump headlong into the Weminuche.

ROCK GLACIER, SAN JUAN NATIONAL FOREST (BOTH PHOTOGRAPHS)

II

WOLF CREEK PASS TO SPRING CREEK PASS

The Weminuche Wilderness

Gay dropped us off at Wolf Creek Pass in the middle of a record heat wave. In Pagosa Springs, where we had taken a day off, it had been almost 100 degrees, and the weather reports we watched on TV in our motel room told us to expect more of the same for the next week. The longer I live at altitude, the more I detest hot weather. A lot of the people I went to college with down in southern New Mexico express incredulity when they hear I now live at 9,600 feet. They simply cannot believe I voluntarily dwell in a town that sees seven months of winter and 300-plus inches of snow per year. But, all I have to do is touch my rump to a billion-degree car seat and hear my flesh fry — which happened in Pagosa every time I got in Gay's car — and I start praying for an immediate Arctic weather front. And Gary, a lifelong Michigander, feels basically the same way. Wolf Creek Pass is 5,000 feet higher than Pagosa Springs, so we knew the temperatures would be blissfully lower. But we also knew that, with a midsummer high pressure system cozily settling in over southwest Colorado, we could expect to sizzle under some scorching high-altitude sun until the weather broke. We stocked up on several gallons of sunscreen before returning to the trail.

As Gay drove off, my heart sank. It's not like she and I are attached at the hip or anything. It's just that Gay is my all-time best hiking partner, and I felt bad about the fact that, while I was pointed with a smile and enthusiasm toward the incomparable Weminuche Wilderness, she was pointed with a frown on her lovely face back toward gainful employment and the endless regimen of bill-paying and housecleaning. She very badly wanted to continue hiking with us, and I wished very badly she could too. This is not exactly the first time in our relationship that I have played out in the woods fairly long term while she toiled back home. She accepts it pretty stoically, but I can't blame her for feeling that, once again, she is getting the short end of the fun-and-frolic stick.

This 120-mile stretch will see us hiking six days to Kite Lake — where Gay and her father will drive a resupply (and, hopefully, several steaks) in to us — then taking a day off, then hiking three more days to Spring Creek Pass. It will be our longest time on the whole hike in between showers. But, the fact that Gay and her dad volunteered to drive all the way in to Kite Lake — which is just south of the middle of nowhere — will make our lives much easier. Instead of having to carry nine days worth of chow from Wolf Creek Pass, the section is now broken down into one six-day stretch and one three-day stretch, with a rest day tossed in for good measure.

Our map situation was much improved over the South San Juans. We were each in possession of a Trails Illustrated topo map of the entire Weminuche, which, at 450,000 acres, is Colorado's largest legally designated wilderness area by far. More importantly, though, Gay and I had hiked from Wolf Creek Pass to Kite Lake two years prior. So, I was perfectly confident there was no way on Earth Gary and I could possibly lose the trail even for a moment — especially because I remembered it being very well marked. At least as far as Kite Lake. After that, I had no idea what turns of the trail we would face. Still, all we would have to do, I told Gary, was keep our wits about us and, surely, we would enjoy an uneventful stroll through the middle of the San Juans, a massive range that many people consider the most beautiful in all of Colorado.

Even though I had already done most of this section, I was still a tad apprehensive as Gary and I lurched away from Wolf Creek under massive packs that were so heavy they seemed to contain full-sized refrigerators. John Fielder summed up the CDT through the Weminuche thus in his book, *The Complete Guide to Colorado's Wilderness Areas*:

Many hikers bail out part way because of weather, fitness or equipment. The trail averages more than 12,000 feet and is exposed to potentially severe weather conditions for almost its entire length. You only dip down below treeline for about an hour during the ten-day journey.

Since I live in the Rockies, I am hardly intimidated by the thought of hiking through altitudinous regions. But the CDT through the San Juans is the kind of trail that grabs the undivided attention even of High Country dwellers. This place is intense, and that intensity is based almost totally on the high-altitude factor, with a side order of extreme remoteness tossed in for good measure. No matter where you hike in the mountains of Colorado, you will eventually find yourself way up high, in the land of pikas and marmots and nosebleeds and acute dizziness. But, in the Weminuche, you stay way up high, day after day, mile after mile. Which is wonderful and all, but the weather here can turn hideous in the blink of an eye. Lightning storms can drop right into your shirt pocket, and they can last for hours. Hypothermia and altitude sickness are constant threats.

All that aside, I was really looking forward to reconnecting with the Weminuche.

The plan was to hike 10 miles from Wolf Creek Pass to Archuleta Lake, a reasonable enough distance after a pizza- and ice-cream-laden day off. It ended up being a lovely walk in and out of several minor drainages, with very little topographical inconvenience. I hardly worked up a sweat. The only problem was the amount of weight I was carrying. My 6,100-cubic-inch-capacity Gregory Robson backpack was filled to brimming. Since I was already starting to gain the appetite that long-distance hikers are infamous for, I had a lot of food with me — something on the order of 5,000 calories per day. Because of the altitude, I was carrying more clothing than usual. And, because of the remoteness of the Weminuche, I was carrying a first aid kit that would do Denver General Hospital's emergency room proud, as well as enough in the way of repair kits with which I could easily service the space shuttle if it landed in our vicinity and needed a complete overhaul. As a result of all this weight, within a half mile from Wolf Creek, my spine started feeling like it was being compressed into one, single, mean-spirited vertebra.

I'm really not sure what Gary was carrying, because we were not sharing gear. Most folks I talked with about this hike assumed that, for weight conservation purposes, Gary and I would be sharing a stove, cook kit, fuel, tent, first aid kit and repair kits. But, since this was the first time either of us had ever done a long hike with a partner, we opted for caution when it came to gear-sharing. We wanted to ensure a degree of independence and privacy, even though such a plan surely added at least 10 pounds of redundant equipment to each of our packs.

We only passed two other people between Wolf Creek and Archuleta Lake — a young couple that had been out for three days. This was our first real chance to assume a macho Divide-Trail-hiker posture, which we figured we were entitled to, since we had made it through the dreaded South San Juans without dying or even getting wounded. Whenever we passed hikers in the South San Juans, we only said we were hiking from Cumbres to Wolf Creek Pass. That way, we would elicit less chuckles from people who might have noticed how hard we were trying to suck our paunches in. But now we were on the verge of being lean and mean, and, without compunction, we told this couple we were hiking all the way to Wyoming. They seemed more jealous than impressed.

It was ridiculously hot and sunny, so we took our time, stopping often to snack, drink, chat and kill mosquitos. Gary had developed some foot problems in the South San Juans, necessitating prolonged rests every two hours or so. As for me, I had exchanged my Fabianos for the pair of Vasque Clarions I had stashed in Gay's car. I also bought some Super Feet insoles and hoped for the best. My blisters were still very painful, but less so with the new footgear.

INDIAN PAINTBRUSH BELOW MOUNT HOPE

Cow elk on the Divide, Weminuche Wilderness

We got to the lake by one o'clock — five hours after leaving Wolf Creek Pass. Because this is a very popular camping area with the spin-casting set, there were several well-defined, level tent sites. As soon as I had my tent set up, I dived face first into my food supply, having decided that I would much rather deal with starvation later on down the trail than deal with a billion-pound pack, as a random example, tomorrow. I even considered eating my clothes.

Gary set his tent up 50 yards away. This had less to do with the fact that we both like our space than it did with the fact that, our first night out, I learned a sobering truth about Gary: He is a world-class snorer, and he commences to saw logs in a serious manner almost instantly after saying nighty-night. Before I've even zipped my tent door closed, his little tent is expanding and contracting like something out of a cartoon, and animals throughout the proximate forest are running for their lives, because, when Gary is snoring, he sounds for all the world like the T-Rex in Jurassic Park. Since I am a near insomniac under the most quiet of circumstances, I had to implore Gary to set his tent up as far away from mine as possible every night. He happily obliged.

This marks the first time Gary and I were alone together in camp and, therefore, it was our first chance to get to know each other a little better. Gay and I met Gary in 1988 while we were all hiking down in the Copper Canyon region of Mexico. Since then, we had got together a couple of times, but we really didn't know him very well. I asked him to join me on this hike because I thought it would be interesting to attempt such a trip with a partner, and I knew that Gary, a 49-year-old of some independent means, would be able to and interested in joining me.

By late afternoon, a fishing pole-carrying family of five arrived via the Archuleta Creek Trail. In addition to bearing visages endemic to occasional hikers on the brink of terminal exhaustion, they looked slightly disappointed that we had already taken the most prime spots. But, after exchanging amicable greetings with us, they proceeded to set up their monster Taj Mahal-esque wall tent across the creek.

Though a few clouds moved through, it stayed hot and dry. I had already consumed more than a gallon of water for the day and, still, I felt dehydrated. For weight purposes, I was not picking up my Katadyn filter until Spring Creek Pass, meaning that I was using (gag) iodinated water for the first 16 days of this hike. Even though I added ascorbic acid (in the form of a product called Potable Aqua-Plus) to the purified water — which mitigates the foul taste and odor of the iodine — it still had the bouquet of Vin de Funky Trail Socks, vintage last century. So, it's sometimes hard to suck down as much water as I should.

We rise at dawn, as usual. I actually feel somewhat liberated this fine morning. While hiking through the South San Juans, I reached a decision that was to have a profound effect on the rest of the hike: I decided that instant oatmeal would never again pass my lips. For many years along many trails, I ate instant oatmeal for breakfast as though it was some sort of price-of-admission-type requirement of

SUNSET ON PIEDRA PEAK

ABOVE SQUAW PASS

backpackers by the Nature Gods. But, I have always detested every single "flavor" of instant oatmeal. I used to buy boxes of instant oatmeal as Christmas presents for people I didn't like.

So, while we were camping at Silver Pass, the night before Wolf Creek, I put my foot down and swore to those Nature Gods that my digestive tract would forevermore be an instant oatmeal-free zone. Of course, that left me with a slight problem: what to eat for breakfast that was light, cheap to cook and filling. After walking up and down every aisle in the supermarket in Pagosa Springs about 20 times — all the while studiously scrutinizing the on-trail breakfast potential of products as disparate as Frosted Pop Tarts, sugar-coated vampire-shaped cereal and cans of corned beef hash — I

ON THE TRAIL

decided to metamorphose into a Cream-of-Wheat man, and, by gollies, while I was eating breakfast at Archuleta Lake, that felt darned good.

That is until I smelled the bacon and eggs being cooked up by our neighbors across the creek. It's astounding how far that particular smell can travel and, even though there is nothing more gross in the entire world than bacon and eggs,

the aroma of bacon and eggs wafting through the woods is one of life's truly wonderful sensations. I had to use a bandana as a bib, to prevent my fairly clean T-shirt from getting soiled by Cream-of-Wheat-laden drool.

From Archuleta Lake, the trail takes a poignant turn skyward, 1,000 feet up the side of Mount Hope. It is an arduous ascent and, once the trail topped out, I lost my breath, in more ways than one. Here, the trail reconnects with the Divide in a peace that drives the concept of the Divide home. For the next dozen or so miles, the trail stays right atop its namesake. Literally, you spill your water off to the right and it makes its way to the Gulf of Mexico. To the left, it goes into the Colorado River and, eventually, the Sea of Cortez.

From Mount Hope, the length and breadth of the Weminuche opened up before us. We could see as far as Rio Grande Pyramid and The Window — two astounding topographic features we will pass in four days. And we will be able to see them coming closer and closer for most of that time. They will serve as an indication of our progress through the San Juans, and this section of trail will be defined as pre-Pyramid/Window and post-Pyramid/Window.

The weather, once again, was clear and hot. Not surprisingly, there is precious little shade above treeline, so we were facing the full brunt of the sun at 12,000 feet. We were both maniacally applying sunscreen, but were sweating so much it was washing off almost immediately, some heading toward the Atlantic, some heading toward the Pacific.

We passed several herds of elk, mule deer and bighorn sheep, as well as numerous ptarmigans, marmots and pikas. The wildflower situation, however, was not up to snuff. When Gay and I had hiked through here two years prior, we hit the best wildflower summer either of us could remember. But, the dryness of this year had taken its toll on the flora situation in the San Juans. The few flowers we passed were small and wilted, and even the tundra grass looked like it could use a good watering. Last winter's snowpack in the San Juans was less than half of average, and there had been precious little rain

BYRON JONES AND COMPANY ON LUNCH BREAK

during the summer. These things go in cycles in the High Country, as, the previous year, the Divide hereabouts had so much snow it did not melt out until the middle of August.

We planned to hike as far as Piedra Pass, which is 12 miles from Archuleta Lake. I was worried that there may not be water along the trail. This is a concern that would be with us for the next few days. I prefer to carry two one-liter water bottles — which I can usually nurse through an entire day in all but the most Sahara-like circumstances — but, because of weight considerations, Gary prefers carrying only one liter.

Gary had also done a fair amount of hiking in the Weminuche, and perspective is at play here. I remembered the hiking as being relatively easy, since, once you get up high, you pretty much stay up high. He remembered the CDT through the San Juans being very difficult, fraught with

ALONG THE TRAIL ON THE DIVIDE

constant, long ups and downs. Being a mountain dweller, I do not consider 2,000-foot ascents that onerous; being a flatlander, Gary considers 2,000-foot ascents to be incredibly challenging and bothersome. We would be averaging at least 4,000 feet of ascents per day for the next 100-plus miles. Gary expressed his trepidation concerning this reality to me several times.

It is true that Gary does not hike uphill well. I watched as he and Gay climbed up the last hill of consequence before we arrived at Wolf Creek Pass,

ALPINE GARDEN, WEMINUCHE WILDERNESS

and they both looked like backpack-toting Sisyphuses. Their muscles were rigid and there was no fluidity to their stride. Uphills, it was clear, were their enemies.

Being not smart, I happen to love uphills, and have worked hard over the years to become a better climber. I have learned to relax my muscles while hiking uphill, and how to pace myself and adjust my stride so as not to exceed my anaerobic threshold. I make certain my shoulders and arms are integrated into the ascension equation, and that my posture is upright and my center-of-gravity balanced. I utilize a lock step, wherein my knees lock just a bit with each stride, and I avoid if at all possible hiking up on my tippy toes, because that's hard on the calves and Achilles tendons. More importantly, though, I have learned to not get psyched out by ascents. I tried to talk to Gary about all this, and, as he ended up telling me many times in many contexts over the course of our CDT hike, he is too old to change.

We ate lunch right on the trail in the middle of a shadeless rock field. Cali crawled behind my pack in a vain attempt to get out of the sun. Being a long-furred, jet-black dog who loves to do things like take naps on snowbanks during sub-zero blizzards, this weather is hitting her hard. I had given her most of my water already, but there was nothing more I could do for her. I suddenly realized I was paying more attention to Gary and Cali than I was to myself. The group leader rides on, into the sunset, perhaps into oblivion.

We continued along the Divide above the wide Goose Creek drainage. We were traveling almost directly west under the intense afternoon sun, and I could hear my nose frying. Sort of smells like bacon. We hadn't passed water since morning and we were both getting low. Finally, after passing South River Peak, we began our final descent of the day, a 2,000-foot drop into Piedra Pass. Fifteen minutes later, we cross a stream about six inches wide, and Cali acts as though it's Lake Superior. As she lays her entire body in the water, working on her backstroke technique, I take my boots off and soak my feet. So far, so good, or at least not so bad, with regard to the Vasque boots and Super Feet insoles. The old wounds are still there, but there has been no new membership in the Fayhee Blister-of-the-Minute Club.

It's still early and we're in no hurry. This is very near where Gay and I camped two years ago, on our eighth anniversary. Then, the valley was lush and green, and there were brilliant flowers of myriad species covering the mountainsides in every direction. (Gay had even sweetly thanked me for the anniversary flowers.) Now, the valley is parched.

It takes another 30 minutes to reach the pass, and — oh joy and rapture — there is a small lake and ample water.

Unfortunately, there's squat in the way of decent campsites. I am inclined to hike on a few more miles up toward the Krummholz Zone, to a point where I remember a mountain stream. But, there's a good chance that the stream will be bone-dry this summer, and, since there's nary a drop of water for at least 10 miles past that point, we opt to stay at Piedra Pass.

TARNS ON THE DIVIDE

BITTER CRESS, WEMINUCHE WILDERNESS

THE WINDOW AND RIO GRANDE PYRAMID

We spent the afternoon involuntarily sunbathing and swatting at the biting flies that had been attacking us in droves ever since we arrived. There's nothing more pleasant that getting bit by a fly on flesh that is already badly sunburned, then smacking the fly, impacting said sunburned skin hard enough to leave a handprint, only to realize that, once again, the fly is not only no longer where you just smacked, but, at that very moment, is removing a large chunk of flesh from yet another sunburned patch of your carcass. And it's too hot to even consider putting on long clothes. I tried to rest in my tent for a few minutes, but, as it was directly in the sun, it was sweltering inside.

Several times, I take Cali down to the lake for a swim. She's beginning to act a little weirded-out, like she's wondering when we're going home. Before this trip, the longest she'd ever been away from the home was four nights. We've already been out 10 nights on this trip, with a mere 52 to go.

Surprisingly enough, the temperature dipped to a nippy 28 degrees during the night. There was so much frost on my tent, I could barely get the door unzipped.

Perhaps it wasn't such a good idea to have forewarned Gary that we were staring down the gullet of the hardest day of the entire Weminuche stretch, the 14 miles from Piedra Pass to Cherokee Lake. Those 14 miles kicked Gay and me very sternly in the ego when we hiked through here.

It ended up that Gary and I could have hiked those few extra miles the day before, because the mountain stream I had remembered still contained water. There wasn't much, but it would have sufficed. Past that point, though, we might as well have been hiking through Saudi Arabia for the next 10 miles, and those 10 miles presented a lot more uphill than down.

We proceeded along the northeast flank of Palomino Mountain before following the Divide up the ridge from hell. This particular ridgeline was sandy, rocky, dry as toast, dusty as a used bookstore and consisted of nothing but steep, knobby false summit after steep, knobby false summit — for five or six miles. Cali's tongue was dragging so far behind her, I tripped over it several times. By the time we reached the end of the Achilles heel-ripping false summit ordeal, I had begun to rethink my uphill hiking opinions. I remembered that, years ago, long before I ever made my peace with uphills, I actually loathed ascending. Each summit felt less like a victory than it did the end of a prison sentence. The analogy of hitting yourself in the head with a hammer sprang to mind.

But, since the last few miles before Cherokee Lake were lovely and level, those thoughts soon faded. Since I am not a big fan of drinking lake water if there is a convenient flowing alternative, we stopped at a small creek three-quarters of a mile short of the lake to fill our water bags. Gary usually only goes through six liters

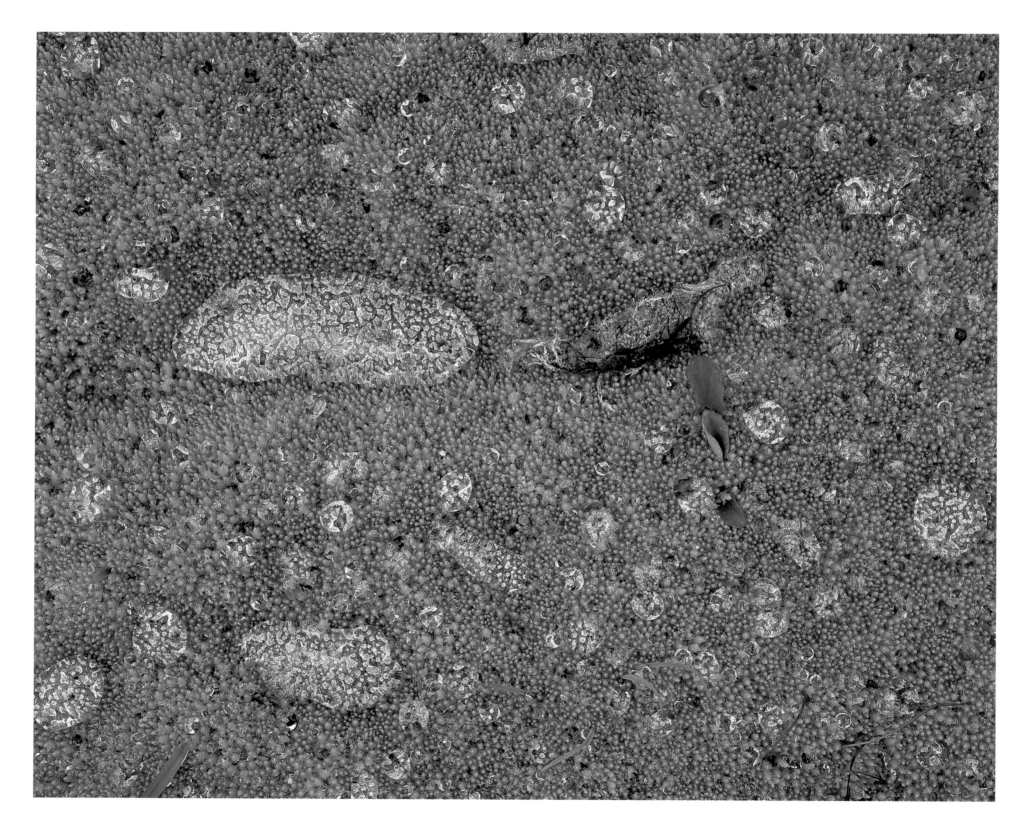

RAINDROPS, WEMINUCHE WILDERNESS

SUNSET OVER THE NEEDLE MOUNTAINS

while in camp, but I use 10 or 12. That translates to 20 or 24 extra pounds. I put my full water bag on top of my pack and, after such a long, hot day, it felt as though the weight of the world had just been dropped onto my shoulders. By the time we reached the lake, I was a staggering mess.

Cherokee Lake is so lovely, it only took a few minutes before I felt revived. The far side of the lake lies under rugged cliffs and rock outcroppings. We were camped between the lake and a 200-foot drop-off into the West Trout Creek Drainage. When Gay and I camped here, she said of that drainage that she had never seen a place that so much lived up to the connotation of wilderness. It truly looked like no person had ever trod there.

I was very concerned that Cali might, while chasing a butterfly or dealing with a doggie hallucination, run right off that cliff, which starts only a few feet from the front of our tent. I kept her close all evening. If Cali dies on this journey, I will have to face the wrath of Gay, and that's something I don't want to do.

It was a transcendent morning, the kind that would have given Whitman a hundred verses, Emerson a dozen essays and Thoreau, being Thoreau, 2,000 pages of journal entries that he somehow would have managed to make laborious to read. We were camped next to a small lake above Squaw Pass at about 12,000 feet. For those of us who are card-carrying Colorado alpine-o-philes, the Weminuche is the best place on Earth. I have let my wife know the Weminuche is where I want my ashes tossed to the four winds when it comes time for me to go meet the Backpacking Buddha, and this is pretty much where I made that decision two years ago.

We were almost halfway through the Wolf Creek Pass-to-Spring Creek Pass section. We were now 11 days out from Cumbres Pass and just getting to the point where trail life feels like life rather than a diversion from life. And I was as much at home as a man can be. So far on this hike, I had been Mister Serious Business. Until now, I had been more focused on the health, well-being and happiness of others — Gay, Gary, Cali — than I had on myself or any other aspect of the journey. But, finally, I was gaining confidence that this hike to Wyoming would, indeed, end in Wyoming. So I felt free that fine morning in that astounding locale to finally let go of my hyper-responsibility act and to open my eyes and let my mind wander free up here in the tundra, the life zone I love above all others. And wander it did, away from the regimen of camp and trail life and the concept of hiking a certain number of miles per day, away from the cooking and dishwashing, the camp-breaking and pack-cinching — to the point where I felt an almost embarrassingly schmaltzy primal bond with this place and the cobalt-skied High Country morning that framed it.

This is turf that would have had morbid Joseph Conrad running for cover. It is the antithesis of the Heart of Darkness; it is, rather, the Heart of Lightness. If I were a bird, I would be tweeting my fool head off out of sheer exuberance. As we hit the

YELLOW PAINTBRUSH, WEMINUCHE WILDERNESS

JOHN FIELDER

VIEWING VESTAL AND ARROW PEAKS

trail, I realized this was one of those rare times when I would not trade my Here & Now for any other Here & Now in the world. Usually, I am the kind of person who, if I am hiking through the Rockies, will be daydreaming about, say, canoeing in Honduras. But this area is so attention grabbing that my mind could not venture to another place if it tried.

We make our way up (and up and up) and over Grouse Rincon. Again we are walking directly atop the Divide. Finally, there are some clouds moving in. Ordinarily, in the middle of a High Country summer, we would get monsooned every afternoon. But, so far, it has been a waste of time even carrying rain gear on this stretch. It looks very much like that may change today. As we descend back down into the trees, we hear thunder off in the distance.

We have decided to go for our first 15-mile day. Ever since I hiked through here with Gay, I have regretted not camping directly below the Window, so Gary agrees to push hard and do just that. If we make it all the way to the base of the Window, it will be our first night camping in the tundra.

We slogged across mile-wide Weminuche Pass, which is essentially one huge bog. Then, we began the long climb toward treeline. I had forgotten just how steep this section was. It took three hours to go 3.5 miles and, just before we passed the last trees, a ferocious thunderstorm moved in. We hastily donned our Gore-Tex and, seconds later, a bolt of lightning hit the ground right in front of me. It is ironic that, though I am the most ardent tundra devotee I know, I am also the world's biggest wimp when it comes to lightning; I cringe at the mere thought of it. I immediately sprinted back down the hill and

took refuge under the closest spruce. There are a lot of people who will say that hunkering down under a tree is the worst thing you can do during a lightning onslaught, but, to those people, I say phooey, or at least some more intense synonym of phooey. It simply feels safer under trees while lightning is popping all around and the thunder is pounding your eardrums before the flash is even done.

As fast as it moved in, the storm moved out, and we were on our way. The sky was not clear, though. It seemed certain more rain would visit us this day. At least for a change it wasn't hot.

Off to our right, Rio Grande Pyramid, at 13,821 feet, loomed large. I'm not certain if the Window, which is just a huge notch in the Divide ridge, had religious significance to the Utes, but, if it didn't, it should have. In addition to being a very prominent and unique feature, it has a weird sense of scale, like most things above treeline. Since there is little in the tundra to use as distance references, it is usually very hard to tell how far away something is, or how big or small it is. Also, I have read that, in places where the air is extremely clear and pollution free, it's harder to gauge distances because distant objects are as in-focus as close objects. From the trail, I couldn't even venture a guess whether the Window was 20 or 500 feet high.

So, we have to rely on metaphor to establish a sense of scale: the Window is big; we are small.

As round two of the thunderstorm moved our way, we passed two gentlemen who were in their 70s. I love seeing senior citizens tromping, packs on back, through the middle of nowhere, and I don't mean that in a condescending way. I just hope I'm still able to carry a pack through the mountains all day when I'm 70. It was interesting to note that they both were carrying revolvers on their hip straps. Maybe they knew something we didn't.

They told us there was a small lake a half hour ahead. By

"CAMP PARADISE"

the time we got there, it was once again pouring and we were being entertained by an extraordinary lightning show. We slid in under some dwarf willows, hoping the storm would pass quickly. After a few minutes, I got up and scouted ahead for a campsite. It ended up that we were only a few feet from a perfect spot right next to the little lake.

We quickly set our tents up and climbed in to escape the rain. Since neither of us was carrying a top-of-the-line tent, we were both worried that the storm, which was getting more intense by the minute, would destroy our flimsy mobile domiciles. As my diminutive single-walled tent was getting

THE CONTINENTAL DIVIDE TRAIL

whipped vigorously around, I swore that this would be my last trip with such an inexpensive one.

In less than an hour, the storm had moved through and the sun broke out. There are few things more wonderful than the High Country right after a summer deluge. The smells were sweet and the tundra-dwelling birds were serenading us with enthusiasm.

After dinner, with the Window looming above us, seemingly only a few feet away, I decided to take a stroll. I was tempted to

Colorado columbine, Weminuche Wilderness

hike up to the Window, but was feeling lazy after 15 miles of hiking. The fact that we had another 15 planned for the next day contributed to my slothfulness. But, soon, I felt myself inextricably and inexplicably drawn to the Window. It was like a magnet. Even though I was only wearing my camp sandals, I started walking toward it. The going was much steeper than it appeared from camp, and it took 45 minutes of steady effort to make it. As soon as I got there, a giant rainbow broke out in the valley far below me, and my shadow and that of the Window appeared right in the middle of that rainbow.

The Window itself was about 50 yards wide and its walls were maybe 200 feet high. It felt like I was in the middle of some sort of cosmic tuning fork. I kept expecting to have a revelation or, failing that, at least to have a deep thought or two. But, all I could come up with was, "Whoa, great view!" Cali was impressed by my insight. To the west, indeed, the view was stupendous — perhaps the best in the entire state. The Grenadiers and the Needles — mountain ranges with well-deserved reputations for beauty and intensity — seemed only a stone's throw away. Tomorrow, we would be hiking past them as we made our way over Hunchback Pass and down into Kite Lake.

Also tomorrow, we would leave the Weminuche Wilderness, and that was both a sad and exciting thought. We had made it without incident, and, the day after Gay and her dad would be meeting us at Kite Lake with food.

I returned to camp, feeling sort of bad that I hadn't invited Gary to hike to the Window with me. But it felt good to be alone, and that's something Gary understands as well as anyone I have ever met.

I also felt bad because this day was my tenth anniversary. This marks the fifth time I have been away on my anniversary day. A 50-percent anniversary absentee rate is not so good. It's a wonder I still have a wife. It would be very nice if I could right now gaze into my spouse's eyes and tell her how much I love her and how much she means to me. Instead, I look up, and there's Gary's homely visage messing up my view of the Divide.

Whenever I hear the word "shortcut," I always cringe. And I should have run like the wind when I heard it this time. We had just hiked by Ute Lake when we passed two backpackers going the opposite direction. It was a couple, and, after chatting for a few minutes, the dreaded word sprang from the mouth of the male. He told us that we could save several miles of hiking, as well as a 1,000-foot drop from Nebo Pass down into Vallecito Creek and a 1,000-foot ascent immediately thereafter up to Hunchback Pass. All we had to do was leave the CDT and take a little trailless shortcut from Nebo Pass along the Divide to Hunchback. Easy as pie, he said. Just did it, he said. Couldn't mess it up if you tried, he said.

I should have conducted a trailside exorcism and removed the word "shortcut" from my inner being as though it was demonic, which, it turns out, it was.

ABOVE THE CLOUDS ON THE DIVIDE, GUNNISON NATIONAL FOREST

When we got to Nebo Pass, it was obvious that the Divide went straight up to the summit of a nameless peak that towered above us. We could see a cairn on the summit, so we "thought" (and I use that term very loosely) "this must be the way." It was so steep that our noses were dragging on the ground as we climbed. It took an hour to top out, and, once we did, we realized the enormity of our mistake. We had left the trail and headed up to the Divide about a mile too soon. If we had stayed on the CDT 20

ON THE TRAIL

more minutes, we could have bypassed this mountain — which ended up being 13,000-plus feet high — altogether. The northwest side of the mountain, which we were now obligated to descend, was one large talus slope. I have pretty good balance, and I considered it one of the most difficult descents I have ever done. I was very concerned about Gary, although he ended up doing just fine. For an hour, we hopped from loose rock to loose rock, hoping against hope that neither of us broke an ankle.

This is when and where my dog lost her sanity.

She totally freaked out — yelping, whining, whimpering and, essentially, begging Daddy to take her home right now. She seemed petrified at the thought of taking another step through this horrendous talus field. I coaxed her down to a fairly level boulder, took her pack, tied it to my pack, and

SIDE HIKE BELOW THE DIVIDE

sternly informed her that this was neither the time nor the place to go nuts.

When we got down, I checked her paws and saw that they were torn up fairly badly. I had been applying a special dog-paw wax to her pads every night and, so far, her feet had held up a lot better than mine. Now they were cut and bleeding in several places. However, if I could walk on mangled feet, so, too, could Cali. She had no choice.

For the next hour, we traversed the tundra. In some places, the going was easy; in some places, it was hard. I kept muttering over and over that I could not believe I had encouraged poor Gary to go along with this shortcut insanity. I mean, some of the worst hiking experiences of my life have transpired while taking shortcuts. Damn shortcuts to hell.

Little did I know the worst was still ahead.

We trudged and trudged, seemingly getting no closer to Hunchback Pass. Finally, we topped out on a small ledge and, there, 200 feet down another terrible-looking talus slope, was the pass and the trail. I was so embarrassed at having put Gary and Cali through this ordeal that I did not even want to break stride. I looked back over my shoulder and Gary was right on my tracks, about 50 feet back. I started down and, 10 minutes later, arrived at the bottom. I looked up, and saw neither hide nor hair of Gary. I assumed that he had stopped for a rest.

I ended up waiting for an hour. Then I yelled till I was hoarse. No response. At 2:15, I decided that, if he did not appear by 2:30, I would hike back up. My watch ticked slowly. At precisely 2:30, I sprinted back up the talus slope, much to Cali's consternation. She was so tired and beat-up and hurting that I almost considered leashing her to my pack while I searched for Gary. But that, I decided, would most likely precipitate a complete loss of pooch marbles.

I was running on pure adrenaline, expecting, when I topped out, to see Gary

EXPLORING

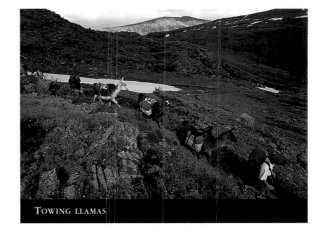

TOWING LLAMAS

lying dead on the rocks, overcome by a heart attack or something. Failing that, I thought that, maybe, he would have his tent set up, making some sort of weird trailside rebellion statement.

But the worst thing imaginable happened: I could not find him. I ran from one end of the knob above Hunchback Pass to the other, yelling as loud as I could the whole time. Cali was whimpering and I had to get stern with her to make her keep up. I was a manic mess. And, still, there was nary a sign of my partner. I simply could not fathom what had happened.

But I knew what must now happen. Hunchback Pass was a little more than a mile from Kite Lake and there is a primitive road to the lake — the very road that Gay and Chuck are supposed to drive in on tomorrow.

I would have to hustle down to the road and hope that there was a compassionate soul there willing to drive me out to the nearest phone, which would be at least 30 rough, dirt road miles away. Then I would have to call search and rescue. I could not believe this turn of events. The temptation to linger for a few more minutes once I got back down to my pack was near-abouts overwhelming. But I had made my decision, and it was the right decision. Just as I was about to pass out of sight of the pass and the talus slope, I took one last look back. I couldn't

JAROSA MESA

believe my eyes. It was Gary, just coming over the lip. I yelled as loud as I could, asking him if he was OK. The only word I could hear from that distance over the wind was "pissed." Apparently, Gary had gotten badly lost and he thought I was to blame.

Trying to cast a good light on yesterday's misadventure, I told Gary that, if that's the worst thing that happens to us on this hike, then we'll be some lucky hombres. I stressed that no one got hurt and all's well that ends well. We talked some things over that we should have talked over before we began the hike. Things about expectations and protocols. By the time Gay and Chuck arrived in the early afternoon, both of us were feeling a lot better about the hike and about our relationship. Perhaps we needed a mishap to get us on the same page.

Cali, sad to say, was spent. After gorging ourselves on steaks, bread and salad, Gay and Chuck had to leave. I sent Cali with them. Less than two hours after arriving, my wife and my father-in-law had to scoot. I almost cried as I sat on an overlook watching them slowly make their way down the Kite Lake road toward the Rio Grande, which was only six miles away.

The next day was among the most intense of my life. From Kite Lake we had eight miles of good trail. Then, it just ended. There were no tread and no signs. I have never used a map and compass that much in my life. We bushwhacked frequently and backtracked often, and we were constantly worried that we were lost. Somehow, though, by 2 p.m., we crossed over into the drainage of the West Fork Pole Creek — right where we were supposed to be. We hiked down the West Fork in a driving rainstorm.

We set up camp on the first semi-flat spot at the intersection of West Fork of Pole Creek and Pole Creek. I was soaked through and shivering uncontrollably. Only after about 10 cups of hot tea did I finally start to warm up. It poured all night and the storm didn't even think about letting up until dawn. We were both miserable and our gear very wet, but as the sun broke out our spirits rose and we had a great day on the trail. We made it 18 miles along the well-marked Colorado Trail — which will be contiguous with the CDT for the next 100 miles — to Big Buck Creek. We were both feeling strong.

We passed at least 20 Colorado Trail hikers going from Denver to Durango. That was more than the total number of people we had seen since Cumbres Pass. At Big Buck, Gary hung out at camp while I went to visit some CT hikers who were camped nearby. While we sat there talking, a full moon rose over nearby Snow Mesa and a herd of at least 400 elk crossed the valley below. It was an astoundingly beautiful, remarkably bucolic scene.

By 11:00 the next morning, we had traversed mellow Jarosa Mesa and arrived at Spring Creek Pass, which was a shock-treatment dose of civilization, as it had a developed campground, a paved parking lot, a kiosk and a very busy highway. Gay was waiting there with Cali, who seemed to have recovered nicely. She seemed to be wondering what took us so long. She wanted to play stick.

DWARF FIREWEED ALONG POLE CREEK

III

SPRING CREEK PASS TO MONARCH PASS

The La Garita Wilderness

For me, the problem with taking time off the trail is that, for every day I spend in town, it takes me an equal number of days to get back into the rhythm of the the walk. After two full days in Lake City, this sad fact was much on my mind as we were making our way through the airy aspen forest on the way up Snow Mesa from Spring Creek Pass. Gay had taken us the 17 miles down from the trail into town, but she had to leave almost immediately to return to Breckenridge. Once again, I saw my wife for less than two hours before Real Life beckoned her home. I opted to send Cali back with her for another week of rest, relaxation and recuperation — so, once again, it was just Gary and me.

A college kid Gary had met in the bar of our motel had driven us back to the trail from Lake City. We arrived at the small Forest Service campground at Spring Creek Pass just before dark and immediately hooked up with a foursome of Colorado Trail through-hikers who were as delightfully debauch as they were wonderfully ill-groomed. They reminded us of us, and we had a great time visiting with them. We stayed up "late" (till almost 10!) swapping lies and telling trail stories. Unlike us, these boys were on the downhill stretch of their journey; since they were coming from Denver, they had only 10 more days before they arrived at Durango, the western terminus of the CT. We, on the other hand, still had 38 days. These trail-weary boys shook their heads sadly and offered condolences. We, in turn, offered condolences to them and speculated that, within about three weeks, they would be missing trail life very badly and expressing anguish over the fact that we were still out in the woods, while they were not. We promised to send them postcards, just to rub it in.

This eight-day, 110-mile stretch — almost all of which follows the Colorado Trail — would see us hiking through the heart of the 130,000-acre La Garita Wilderness, as well as passing through the extremely remote and surprisingly rugged Cochetopa Hills. The La Garita is one of the lesser known wilderness areas in the state. Yet, it is magnificent and wind-swept and wild. Its lack of renown probably stems from its proximity to the much larger Weminuche, as well as the fact that it is home to only one 14,000-plus-foot mountain — San Luis Peak — and, wilderness areas in Colorado are, ridiculously enough, popular in direct proportion to the number of "fourteeners" they harbor. (Witness the sparse use of the South San Juan Wilderness, which is home to no fourteeners.)

It was two miles and less than 1,500 vertical feet from Spring Creek Pass to the top of Snow Mesa. Those are some easy numbers, even when factoring in a full-pack fatigue quotient. Yet, I thought someone had slipped a liter of grain alcohol and three libriums into my morning coffee. I felt dizzy, disoriented and mightily fatigued. I was very happy we only had 11 miles to hike this day, as I didn't feel like I could make it much more than that. Gary was feeling none too chipper himself.

Our days-off gluttony-based sins are catching up with us. Basically, while in Lake City, we mowed down every calorie that had the misfortune of crossing our paths. This we did not do just to keep our jaws limbered up. In 15 trail days, I have dropped 20 pounds, and Gary has dropped almost as much. Our heretofore snug-fitting garments are now hanging loose upon our emaciated carcasses. We could pass for Bataan Death March survivors, except that our clothes are too dirty and tattered. Such rapid weight loss is rough on a metabolism used to carrying some extra weight around; thus, we are now constantly hungry. Food dominates a high percentage of our thoughts. It's like — "Hey, nice view. Doesn't that mountain remind you of a pile of ice cream? And look at those lovely wildflowers; I wonder if they're edible."

It took a long, slow hour to top out on Snow Mesa, which is one of the most splendid parts of the state. This is my third time up here and, every time, I have regretted the fact that I forgot my polo and croquet gear. Snow Mesa is almost 30 square miles of very lush, grassy tundra. By the standards of this neck of the woods, it is flat as a tabletop, and the views from its expanse are astounding in every direction. To the west, we saw the rugged, often storm-ridden section of the Divide where lies Coney Summit — at 13,334 feet, the highest point along the Colorado Trail — and the bright crimson expanse of Red Mountain, the side of which looks like a mammoth wound on the ridge. To the northwest are two of Colorado's most beautiful and dissimilar fourteeners — flat-topped and green Uncompahgre and pointy, forbidding Wetterhorn (both of which I have climbed). And, to the east, we have the heart of the La Garitas.

The "trail" — which consists of nothing more than three-foot-tall plastic markers pounded into the tundra every 50 or 100 yards — spends five leisurely miles crossing Snow Mesa. In addition to enjoying the constant views that are as good as any in the Rockies, we were pleasantly surprised to come across a fair amount of water. A high percentage of the Colorado Trail hikers we passed in the last few days lamented the lack of water between Spring Creek Pass and Monarch Pass. We even met two young men who had hitchhiked around this section because of their fears of parched

ELEPHANT HEAD NEXT TO THE TRAIL, SNOW MESA

throats and swollen tongues. After tromping through many miles of thirsty territory on this hike, Gary and I were not happy with this news. We were specifically told that Snow Mesa was almost totally dry, and what little water there was hereabouts was cattle-polluted beyond drinkability.

I guess Gary and I had developed broader definitions of what was and was not potable on this hike. Ended up there were several small tarns and creeks on Snow Mesa, each of which seemed perfectly fine by us. We hoped our fears about lack of water throughout this stretch would be equally without merit. This is when we started thinking of this year's batch of CT hikers as less than tough.

Actually, our water situation from here on in would be quite different than it had been, as we both had dumped our iodine in favor of our Katadyn filters. In one sense, it is only a coincidence that we own the same type of filter; but, in another sense, it is not coincidental at all, as Katadyn makes the very best (and by far the most expensive) model in the world and, when it comes to keeping hideous protozoans, bacteria, viruses and miscellaneous spooge from visiting our bowel regions while we are out and about in the middle of nowhere, Gary and I are both inclined to own and operate the very best technology. This belief was underscored by the very lad who drove us from Lake City to Spring Creek Pass. Earlier in the summer, he had contracted a case of giardia lamblia — the most prevalent and dreaded form of stomach malady in the High Country — by way of consuming untreated/unfiltered water that he pulled from a pristine-looking mountain stream. He was camping the night the symptoms manifested themselves, and he had to run into the woods (get this) 30 times! I wince just thinking about it. He said it was a thoroughly unpleasant experience, and we believed him to the point that we almost sang out "Hallelujah" as he was relating this tale of intestinal woe. (Giardia is a protozoan passed from warm-blooded carriers like beavers and cows to water sources via feces. Its incubation period is 9–14 days.)

Shortly after crossing the headwaters of a side canyon of Oso Creek, we entered the La Garita Wilderness. We stopped to snack, sip and admire a heart-flutteringly gorgeous view of Uncompahgre and Wetterhorn — 30 miles away — through a window-like notch in the Divide before reluctantly moving on. This day, every step is hard. On long hikes, there are those days, just as there are days when the miles pass almost effortlessly.

As we were climbing up from Snow Mesa, we both realized how comfortable we had become rubbing elbows with the Divide, which is strange indeed, as, historically, the Continental Divide is probably considered the most notorious geological feature in the Rockies. For centuries, the exploration and settlement of Colorado was framed in a context that was centered along the Divide. Trappers, miners, mappers and merchants all spent considerable time and effort for generations dealing with the inconvenience and danger offered up in spades by the backbone of the Rockies in order to conduct their business. Perhaps in the recreation-crazed late 1990s, the fourteeners have usurped the Divide as the state's most ominous and, therefore, most exciting terrain feature in the minds of backcountry enthusiasts. But, only since the '60s have people looked at the fourteeners as anything except tall mountains that, thankfully, are easily avoided as one is traveling around the plague whenever possible, the Divide was considered Colorado's challenge nonpareil. And here Gary and I are stupidly thinking in terms of being buddy-buddy with this awesome topographical anomaly. Yet, we both understand full well that, though we may now feel a familiarity-based karmic bond with the Divide, it remains impassive toward us. That is the way Nature works, even when nice guys like us are factored into the survival equation. I guess it's like drinking with a dragon — everything's hunky-dory right up until the moment when the fire starts flying. We know we cannot afford to feel too comfortable with the Divide no matter how many miles we touch it and are touched by it.

It was just past noon, and, with only four miles left to the Middle Fork of Mineral Creek, where we planned to camp, we had been looking forward to being able to take our time. Then we notice a vicious-looking storm about to break over us like a gaseous tsunami. Since we were at 12,400 feet in the middle of an endless stretch of tundra, we were about as exposed to the elements as two people with all their clothes on can get. So we started nervously quick-stepping our way along the side of the Divide ridge, hoping once again that this was not the day we were destined to interface directly with a bolt of lightning. As we crossed into the Mineral Creek drainage, the storm hit full tilt. There was nowhere to hide. We just kept our fingers crossed and walk on, feeling like a mouse in a snake's cage.

From the West Mineral Creek headwaters, the trail drops back into the trees and into and out of several small, steep drainages. We pass a couple of serious cowboy-looking horsepackers — replete with chaw dribble making its way down their chins. They nod, their black hats pulled down low on their faces. Shortly thereafter, we pass a lone Colorado Trail hiker and his dog. He's a lean man in his early 20s, and he is flat-out flying to Spring Creek Pass. We exchange about 10 words, nine of which have to do with how much food he is going to consume while in Lake City. Before I can issue a warning, he is gone.

The storm let up, and I was feeling a lot more energetic than I had been in the morning. I was several hundred yards ahead of Gary when, suddenly, I rounded a bend and, right there in the middle of the trail, a couple is involved in a bit of what looked to be mouth-to-mouth resuscitation practice. I tried to act innocent, like I didn't see a thing, which was a tough act, as I almost tripped over these two people. We all sort of red-faced chuckled it off, exchanged a couple of weather-related pleasantries, and parted ways. I'm certain that, for years to come, this couple will be telling their friends about how, in the middle of the La Garita Wilderness, a scuzzy-looking Divide Trail hiker walked up on them as they were smooching. I laughed for the next two miles.

Eroded volcanic ash, Miners Creek

We arrived in early afternoon at a promising-looking campsite at the base of a beautiful sheer cliff face and next to a couple of beaver ponds. Since the storm was moving back in again, we decided without compunction to drop our packs and pitch our tents. Almost immediately, though, we realized how trashed by horses this otherwise lovely spot was. We thought back to the two cowboys we had passed on the trail, and, since the ashes in the firepit were still warm, we suspected they were the culprits responsible for the sad state of this campsite — or at least the most recent culprits. There were empty beer and sardine cans, cigarette butts and horse droppings everywhere. (It's tough to feel sympathetic toward anyone who, given the luxury of carrying in via horseback any food item in the world, would choose cans of sardines.) And the animals had been allowed to trample the camp's entire periphery into a muddy pulp.

I try to retain a positive attitude toward horses and the creatures who own and drive them, but, man oh man, it is very hard sometimes. Many miles of the CDT through southern Colorado have been decimated by horse traffic. Not only is this part of the state dominated by ranchers (and thus horses), but it is ground zero for the state's guided-horseback-tour industry. These tours usually consist of two or three tough-looking, no-nonsense wranglers accompanied by anywhere from six to 15 flabby customers who more often than not are dressed in the height of dorky drugstore cowboy fashion — something that I am certain is never mirthfully discussed by the wranglers among themselves back in the bunkhouse.

Because of the heavy horse traffic, the condition of the Divide Trail through the Weminuche and parts of the La Garitas is as bad as I have ever seen. In many places, the tread is eroded down several feet, so it looks from a distance like you are hiking along knee-deep in Mother Earth. There are many other areas that sport four or five distinct trails, all either caused by horses or by hikers bypassing sections of trail damaged by horses. Since the trail in many places could have been named the Continental Divide National Horse Manure Trail, the biting fly situation was often hard to handle.

Over the years, I have hobnobbed with more than a few horsepackers about all this (which is a wonderful way to practice one's self-defense capabilities), and, unfortunately, have never got very far in my attempts to convince them that the damage they cause to trails outweighs that caused by any other user group — except off-road vehicles — by a factor of 10 and, therefore, they should get off of their high horses and do "something" about the situation. I have asked cowboys and horsepackers why they do not spend more time working on volunteer trail crews, at least as a symbolic, good will-type gesture. Time and time again I have been reminded by these people that they have to buy Special Use Permits from the Forest Service to operate their tours and run their cattle and sheep on public lands, and they look at those permits as their tickets to pretty much do as they please. If they cause damage to trails, then, by God, let the Forest Service take care of the problem.

ELEPHANT HEAD BELOW THE DIVIDE, RIO GRANDE NATIONAL FOREST

PHOTOGRAPHING FLOWERS

The thing is, in the West, horses are, well, sacred cows. The Forest Service has come up with a set of Leave No Trace kinds of rules governing how horsepackers ought to operate in the backcountry but, to the best of my knowledge, there has never been any serious effort to limit the number of horses allowed to pass on any given stretch of trail in any given year. Yet, judging from the condition of the CDNST through this part of the state, something needs to be done fast on the regulatory front, lest this budding trail connecting Mexico with Canada simply erodes away right under our feet — and hooves.

We were crashed out well before dark. We were going to bed earlier and earlier every night. If there had been anyone to be embarrassed in front of besides Gary, I would indeed have felt a little sheepish about turning in at 6:30 in the dead of summer. But the physical act of carrying a pack up and down mountains all day is tiring beyond belief. I don't know how any activity could be more tiring in both the immediate and cumulative senses. Factor in the tedious camp part of trail life, and you have a world-class formula for marrow-deep constant fatigue. I slept like I was dead.

The next day was to be the shortest one of our entire hike. We would go only as far as the last water before San Luis Peak, which we would ascend the day after that. The six miles between camp and that last water, however, were cardiovascularly very captivating. There were four extremely steep, essentially trailless up and downs, and, since we crossed the 13,000-foot mark twice, we weren't exactly sprinting. Still, by

11 a.m., we arrived at a lovely campsite. Unfortunately, it was only about six inches from the trail, which, I understand, is a Forest Service regulation no-no, but that's just the way it works out sometimes. This was a spot that had obviously been used as a campsite before and, therefore, it was already impacted. The undergrowth had been smooshed and the soil was compacted. I have done a lot of journalistic research on the subject of minimum impact/Leave No Trace camping, and I know that, sometimes, Forest Service regulations that were designed to protect the environment from the inadvertent actions of otherwise well-meaning backpackers are sometimes self-defeating. The most severe negative impact to any campsite occurs the first time it is used. The second-highest amount of impact occurs the second time it is used. And so on. I would rather break a Forest Service regulation (for mainly social reasons, you're supposed to be something like 200 feet away from the closest trail) than tromp off across the tundra and lay some new impact on a place that never before has seen a tent. The downside of this strategy, of course, is that, because several groups of hikers passed by, this wasn't the most private campsite in the world.

By the time I returned to camp with a full water bag from a close-at-hand, small snowmelt stream, Gary had transformed his part of our campsite into Home Sweet Home. I am envious of his ability to do this. My camps always end up looking like places hobos would earnestly avoid. I have stuff strewn everywhere, and my tent is usually at a 30-degree angle. This is certainly not by design. To the contrary, I've chewed my mental cud over this for years, and have even tried once or twice to make better camps. To no avail. I guess that, subconsciously, I look at campsites as the trail equivalent of interstate highway rest areas. Since I am only going to be here for 12 or 14 hours, there's no reason to get too emotionally attached to the place.

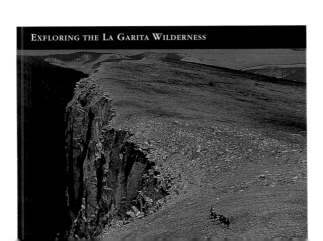

EXPLORING THE LA GARITA WILDERNESS

DAWN LIGHT

Gary's camps, on the other hand, look like they were set up by someone's grandmother. I kept expecting him to have a lawn and garden planted and a little white picket fence erected every day. Gary is adept at psychically bonding with the places where he hangs his hat for the night, and that reality is made evident by the way his camps look. He is, by nature, a nest-builder. His tent sites always look infinitely more cozy than mine, and, while in camp, he always looks more comfortable than I do, even though I carry a backpackable chair and he

JOHN FAYHEE

GAY GANGEL-FAYHEE

does not. He has routines and systems and a sense of in-camp calm orderliness that I could not develop if I dedicated the rest of my days trying. Martha Stewart would love camping with Gary; she would, on the other hand, look at my campsites as being located decidedly on the wrong side of the tracks.

There is no doubt that Gary has the camping part of trail life down better than I, while I have the trail part of camping life down better than he. This, I guess, is simply another example of our personality dissimilarities. He has lived in the same abode — which he built — in Michigan for 20-something years. In that time, I have had 34 different residences,

and only in my 40th year did I buy my first house. I would call myself a nomad by nature, except that nomads are usually very adept at quickly making their campsites very homey. I guess I am more of a wanderer than a nomad.

Not surprisingly, Gary is a lot more content than I am to hang out in camp. He loves getting off the trail early in the day; I, on the other hand, start getting bored and antsy about 20 minutes after pitching my tent. Gary can sit there for hours just staring at a cliff; and, though I certainly appreciate the beauty of a cliff as well as the next man, I generally while away idle camp hours by doing something — reading, writing, repairing gear, taking short strolls or sleeping. I have trouble just sitting; I always have.

We hit the trail shortly after dawn. The Divide ridge was blocking the sun and it was very cold. The plan was to hike up to a small saddle at the head of Cochetopa Creek, drop our packs, ascend San Luis Peak, then hike as far down Cochetopa Creek as we were able. The weather, however, was looking funky. Whenever there are early morning clouds in the Colorado High Country sky, that's usually a bad sign. And today there were banks of clouds moving in from both the south and the west — double jeopardy, as it were. Ordinarily, I would have taken one look at the sky and blown off any thought of ascending a fourteener. But, as far as I know, I am the only person to have hiked the Colorado Trail end-to-end who has not ascended San Luis Peak. When I came through here on the CT five years ago, it was storming badly, and I did not consider for a moment going up. This go-round, I was going to climb the peak, no matter how ill-advised or potentially fatal my attempt might be.

If you happen to already be at the point where we dropped our packs, San Luis Peak is one of the easiest fourteeners in the state. It's only about a mile and 1,500 vertical feet to the summit. If all went well, we could be up and down in less than two hours. The rocky route is marked by cairns, and the first part of the ascent was steep and slow. But, once we achieved the summit ridge, it was a piece of cake. It was only at this point that I started thinking about the superlative shape I was in. Yesterday we went over the 200-mile mark and, by this point on any long hike, you should have your trail legs very much under you. I did not even break stride on my way to the summit, and even Gary, who is still at constant odds with uphills, pretty much breezed his way up. As I was waiting for him at the summit, I realized this was the first time I had ever been alone atop a fourteener. Even though the wind was so strong it was blowing the taste right out of my mouth, I could not remember ever being happier. I guess if you love the tundra as much as I do, then summiting a fourteener is the ultimate experience. "Closer to God" is how one friend of mine described the thrill of sitting on a summit. I have always looked at it as the exact opposite: "Farther above the rat race."

I sat for a moment and ran my fingers along the bright-red and greenish yellow lichens that decorated the rocks on the summit like haphazard paint splashes. Surely the tears I felt running down my face were caused by the incessant wind.

My solitude-based reverie was short-lived, as, within 10 minutes, a couple coming up the Stewart Creek Trail joined me. Gary arrived shortly thereafter. By this point, the wind was gusting to about 50 miles per hour, and those two cloud banks were looking nastier by the minute. We took each other's pictures and sprinted back down to the trail. Our round-trip had taken 1 hour, 45 minutes.

By the time we got down, there were 15 other people getting ready to go up San Luis. We couldn't believe it, as San Luis Peak is one of the most remote fourteeners in the state. But, fourteener-bagging has become a passion in Colorado. Type-A types spend considerable time and effort trying to "knock off" all 54 of our fourteeners, usually for athletic, rather than aesthetic, reasons.

San Luis marked my fourteenth fourteener, and, every time I ascend one, I feel a pang of guilt, because there is little doubt that the fourteener-bagging craze is causing a lot of negative environmental impact on Colorado's loftiest peaks. People like me are leaving muddy bootprints in the temple.

Lightning began to flash in the distance, and I warned the people getting ready to go up about the weather. Every single one of them looked at me quizzically. They hadn't given the weather a moment's thought and evidently didn't plan on doing so. I shook my head as I hoisted my pack. Almost every year in Colorado, people are killed by lightning while bagging fourteeners. But most people subscribe to the act-of-God theory of survival. If God has decided that your time is up, it doesn't matter if you're scaling a mountain or sitting at home watching TV; and, if God has decided that your time is not up, it matters not one iota if you're on top of a peak in the heart of a thunderstorm. Ignorance is truly bliss, right up until the moment your carcass gets fried by a lightning bolt.

The descent into Cochetopa Creek was a major transitional time on our hike. This is when and where we left the San Juan Mountain complex — which includes, among other ranges, the South San Juans, the San Juans and the La Garitas. We now had five days of relatively low hiking before we entered the mighty Sawatch Range, home of Mount Elbert and Mount Massive, Colorado's two highest peaks. We would follow Cochetopa Creek for 15 downhill miles and, as we made our way toward the Eddiesville Trailhead, we suddenly found ourselves nearing the 9,000-foot level for the first time on this hike. You know you've been traversing some lofty terrain when you look at 9,000 feet as lowlands, but that's exactly what we were doing. By the time we left the La Garita Wilderness, it was 85 degrees with perfectly clear skies. We were now 600 feet lower than my house in Breckenridge. It's weird to think that, only three hours before, we were atop San Luis Peak in a gathering gale with the temperature hovering around freezing.

This was the most tired I had been on this hike. We agreed to stop at the first decent-looking campsite after we left the wilderness but, unfortunately, we had to hike several miles before anything even remotely level presented itself. Not only was I dragging, but I was also getting a brand-new set of blisters. Those new Super Feet insoles I bought in Pagosa Springs were already starting to go, and the only part of my feet that had not been blister-infested back in the South San Juans — the blades of my heels — were now completely raw. I tried in vain to stoically walk without limping, grimacing and moaning. I don't know why it's so important to me as a person and as a backpacker to maintain this impassive on-trail demeanor while I'm in near-mortal agony, but it is.

Between the heat, the fatigue and the blisters, I was in a sour mood, and the fact that I have always felt there is no excuse for bad moods out on the trail made me feel even more surly. Once we found a campsite, I quickly dropped my pack and ran down to the creek. Since we were so low, the water is not as cold as usual, and

for the first time since Cumbers, I completely immersed myself. After a few minutes, I started to feel better. I have always been amazed at the curative powers Mother Nature boasts in both the short and long terms. Back home, it would have taken many hours and many aspirins to extricate myself from such a foul mood.

Still, I fell into bed shortly after dinner. But I did not sleep well, as the night air was constantly shattered by the grating noise of jets passing overhead. This was eerie on several levels. First, we hadn't noticed many planes up to this point on our journey. All of a sudden, out here in middle of one of the most remote parts of the state, we have happened under the major flyway. But more than that was the nature of the noise. Whenever a plane flew over, it was more than 15 minutes between the time the first dull rumble came over the hill and the time the noise finally dissipated. It was like we were at the heart of some sort of auditory vortex. This went on all night, one plane after another and, basically, this went on for the next 200 miles. I had no idea there were so many planes crossing Colorado's lustrous skies.

BEAVER PONDS ON COCHETOPA CREEK

69

ALPINE CAMP, LA GARITA WILDERNESS

TARN BELOW THE CONTINENTAL DIVIDE

I had been dreading this day's hike ever since we left Cumbres Pass. Once we left Cochetopa Creek, we had to traverse 10 hot, dusty, shadeless, waterless miles through Saguache Park, and every one of those miles followed hard-packed Jeep trails. Even the best dirt roads wreak havoc on the feet when you're carrying a backpack, and these were not the best dirt roads. They were rutted and rocky, presenting ample opportunity for twisted ankles and stone bruises. By the standards established by the trail so far, the views were nonexistent. But, at least those 10 miles were mostly level, and we arrived shortly after noon at Los Lake, the last water before North Pass, where Gay was to meet us with a food drop the next day.

When all those Colorado Trail hikers were griping about the lack of water along this stretch, Los Lake was the epicenter of their descriptive venom. Verily, it was not the sort of water source around which you would likely plan a vacation, and its image will never adorn a scenic calendar. It was a small, well-trampled stock pond that had much evidence of recent mass bovine visitation, but, once again, Gary and I ended up pooh-poohing the toughness of the CT hikers we had talked to on the subject of water. Los Lake just wasn't that bad.

Still, Los Lake made us truly appreciate having water filters instead of iodine. Though it took me almost 45 minutes to filter enough water to see me through an afternoon, evening and morning, at least, once the chore was done, I had three gallons of clear, fresh-tasting and odorless agua. If we had to rely on iodine at a place like Los Lake, the water would end up tasting like cream of mud soup.

The only real problem with camping near Los Lake centered around the unbelievable numbers of cow pies (though, surprisingly, there were no cows to be seen). And these were some healthy cow pies. I was thinking in terms of contacting the Guinness Book of World Records. I don't know what the cows eat around here, but they eat a lot of it. We literally could not move without coming into contact with cow droppings. If you had the misfortune of stepping into one of these monstrosities, you would easily sink up to your knee. After a few hours, we started getting comfortable with all the cowpies; we started thinking of them as decorations or even furniture. It got to the point that we were using them as ashtrays and water bottle holders.

After a beautiful and easy 8-mile stroll through a dry but sun-dappled section of long-abandoned, leaf-covered timber roads, we arrived at North Pass. Gay and Cali were waiting for us, exactly as planned.

Gay drove us 30 miles into Saguache for a plateful of unbelievably greasy and delicious Mexican food and to see if I could buy some new insoles. Gary had given me a spare pair at Los Lake. (Yes, he actually had a spare pair of insoles in his pack; Martha Stewart would be proud.) Since his feet are twice as big as mine, I had to cut them down to size. Though they felt a lot better than the now completely deformed Super Feet insoles, I needed to get something better fast. Saguache isn't exactly Manhattan, and the closest thing I could find to insoles at the local three-aisle grocery store was a pair of size-5 Odor Eaters. Not exactly what I needed.

HEADWATERS OF SAGUACHE CREEK, LA GARITA WILDERNESS

COLORADO COLUMBINE ON THE DIVIDE

WHEELER GEOLOGIC AREA

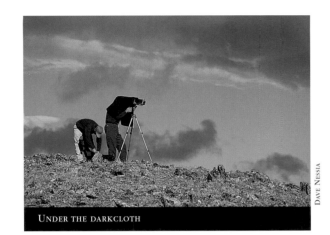
UNDER THE DARKCLOTH

DAVE NESSIA

I resigned myself to limping three more days on Gary's old insoles to Monarch Pass. From there, we planned to take a day off in Salida, a town that has several backpacking stores, where, surely, I could deal with my feet/insole problems once and for all. The good thing about all these blisters is that I am developing one tough set of toe-to-heel callouses. In another couple of weeks, I will be able to walk barefoot if need be.

There are only three dependable water sources through the little-visited Cochetopa Hills between Highway 114 and Monarch Pass, so we had to plan our hiking days accordingly. Two days past North Pass, this meant setting up camp after a very short and easy day on the side of Tank Seven Creek, a lovely babbling brook about two feet wide and six inches deep. It was such a prototypically beautiful Colorado summer day neither one of us minded in the least parking it early. As I was sitting in my Crazy Creek camp chair reading, with the birds tweeting, the creek gurgling and Cali, who had rejoined us at North Pass, wrestling with a stick, I realized how completely relaxed I was. All the civilization-based detritus that felt like a vise around my noggin back when we started this hike 26 days ago was now a distant memory. I felt totally liberated from the shackles of workaday life for the first time in many years. The hard exercise and the absorbing demands of trail life certainly had a lot to do with that. But I believe

those aforementioned curative powers that Mother Nature possesses were most responsible for my current tranquil state of being.

Just as I lit up the afternoon's third cigar (a three-stogie day is a good day indeed), up walked two older gentlemen who looked like they had just jumped out of the pages of a 1974 REI catalogue. They had near-ancient external-frame packs, blue jeans, flannel shirts and, yes, even Sierra cups on their belts. We chatted for a few minutes, and, since we had the best campsite on Tank Seven Creek, we invited them to join us for the evening.

The first man introduced himself as Delray Green. As the second man extended his hand, my jaw dropped.

"Hi, I'm Jim Wolf," he said.

Two full days from the closest trailhead in a little-used part of the state, I had just made the acquaintance of the father of the Continental Divide Trail. I didn't know whether to bow, genuflect or offer him a cigar. (It ended up he had his own.) Wolf was on a three-week CDT reconnoitering trip, and we enjoyed a pleasant evening talking about the trail.

I coaxed from him the story of the CDT and his long-lived relationship with it.

Wolf, a Baltimore resident who was born in 1930, is a lawyer by trade, spending most of his career working for the Nuclear Regulatory Commission. He developed his passion for the Continental Divide while he was a child, and that passion is part of him still.

"As a kid, every summer, I went off to camp," he said.

CAMP

"One summer, I went to a ranch camp in Idaho near Yellowstone. I fell in love with the West. While I was in law school, I became an avid bird-watcher, which, in turn, led to associations with other kinds of outdoorspeople. I started getting more involved in the outdoors. I ended up taking several trips out West. One of those was a 10-day trip into the Wind Rivers. That was my first contact with the Divide. In 1971, I hiked the entire Appalachian Trail, which instilled in me a love of long-distance trails."

"When I finished the AT, I started

ON THE DIVIDE AT 13,400'

thinking about what adventure I wanted to do next. I heard that there was a study underway by the Bureau of Outdoor Recreation to see if there were any other trails that should be added to the National Scenic Trails Act. I started studying the possibility of putting a Divide Trail route together. I decided to make it my goal to show that a route could be established from Canada to Mexico basically following the Divide."

By the time Congress was considering amending the National Scenic Trails Act, Wolf had hiked all the way to Mexico.

"I went out West every summer and worked on it," he says. "But the goal was not just to put any route together. I wanted it to include as much scenery and cultural sites as possible. I knew, if Congress ever established the trail, that it would not end up following my route exactly. I just wanted to come up with a baseline or benchmark that would help the land stewardship agencies determine the route. I wanted to put together an interim route that people could use while the official route was being established."

It was Wolf who first scouted most of what has become the CDT's route through Colorado.

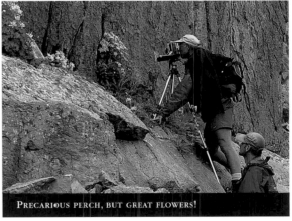
PRECARIOUS PERCH, BUT GREAT FLOWERS!

DAVE NESSIA

The unfortunate thing is that, despite all of his efforts, Wolf is on the verge of becoming irrelevant vis-a-vis the CDT. The Continental Divide Trail Society, which he founded almost 20 years ago, is being displaced by the newer, slicker, more heavily funded Continental Divide Trail Alliance, which has nothing to do with Wolf. When I asked Jim about this situation there on the side of Tank Seven Creek, he politely changed the subject, preferring to hear my observations about the parts of the trail we had hiked.

We arrived at Marshall Pass, which once was home to the state's second-highest railroad, in the middle of a thunderstorm. Though there are several nice campsites right next to the gravel road that crosses the pass, I knew from previous travels in the area that there was a small, primitive cabin only about five minutes from the trail. I'm not the biggest fan of musty old mouse-infested cabins, but I knew Gary would be very pleased. Truth be known, Gary would be perfectly happy if such cabins were strategically stationed along the entire length of the CDT. There has long been talk among folks (who should move without further ado back East) about establishing a series of backcountry shelters along the Colorado Trail. This is something I oppose so vociferously that I cannot even get on the subject without getting a headache and turning even more contrary than usual. Surely, sooner or later, someone will propose the same sort of thing for the CDT. Why can't people just leave well enough alone? Why is there this constant urge among humans who ought to know better to build things in the middle of the boonies, all for purposes of "comfort?" If people want comfort, then let them stay at home, or, failing that, go hiking in the White Mountains of New Hampshire, where there already exists a fine series of backcountry huts. Leave Colorado's backcountry alone.

But, I must say, I certainly did appreciate the shelter that vacant cabin at Marshall Pass provided.

This cabin, which is open to the public, was the base of operations for a cattle camp back in the '30s and is preserved and maintained by a Salida-based snowmobile club. It offered a table, a woodstove (which Gary used to heat water for a full-blown bath), a nearby creek and, most importantly, a roof. Since the one bed was ratty looking beyond belief, I magnanimously offered it to Gary. I opted to pitch my tent and sleep out in the fresh air, where I belong and am most happy.

A few minutes after I set my tent up though, the summer's most intense rainstorm hit. By the time it moved on, the inside of my tent and my down sleeping bag were soaked. I spent a long, uncomfortable night, and Cali simply could not believe that, with a dry cabin 50 feet away, we were trying unsuccessfully to snooze in a completely saturated tent. I let her out a couple of times, and she ran up and sat on the cabin's porch, whimpering.

I felt much better when I learned the next morning that Gary had been kept up all night by rodents scurrying around the cabin. He reported that several had even scampered across his face.

After a tough four-mile ascent through thick woods, we topped out on the Divide once again, and, shortly after passing treeline, we left the Colorado Trail. (We would hook back up with it in six days.) It was like parting ways with a good friend. But, we had gotten spoiled by the high quality of the CT, which is well signed and pretty much manicured every step of the way. It was time to get back on trail that was CDT and CDT only, for better and for worse.

For four miles we stayed up high, following beautiful trail that was almost bumper-to-bumper mountain bikes. We passed at least a dozen cyclists, 10 of whom were completely rude. I am an avid mountain biker, so I try to cut mountain bikers a little slack because, like snowboarders, they are often on the receiving end of a lot of ill-deserved snobbery and bad press. Still, I believe every mountain biker ought to bend over backward to serve as an ambassador for the sport. That includes following the established protocol (silly as that protocol is) by dismounting and yielding to hikers, as well as exchanging at least basic friendly greetings with other trail users. Only two of the bikers we passed on this stretch of trail yielded to us. The rest were not only bad-mannered, but they were extremely unfriendly as well. Not one said hello, and most went out of their way to turn their noses upward as they passed. I was tempted to jam a branch through several sets of passing spokes but, since we were above treeline, branches were in very short supply.

As we began our descent into Monarch Pass and U.S. Highway 50, we passed a series of wonderful cairns, which were totally unnecessary, because the tread was so good. These cairns were erected by people who obviously took their cairn-building very seriously. Heretofore, all of the cairns we had passed — and we had passed thousands — were not exactly works of art. They were little more than piles of rocks, which is pretty much what cairns are. But the cairns above Monarch Pass all looked like miniature headstones. It was like we were passing through one serpentine cemetery.

I hoped this was not some sort of divine sign.

A half mile before Monarch Pass, we started hearing the racket. At Monarch Pass, there is a gaudy tourist facility, replete with a tram, museum and gift shop. Since it was Saturday, there were hundreds of cars parked there.

One of them belonged to my father-in-law, who, immediately upon laying eyes on our emaciated selves, let us know that, right next to the museum entrance, there was a hot dog stand selling $2 bratwursts. I had $10 cash in my wallet when I walked up to that stand. I had zero dollars when I walked away.

We were now halfway through our trip.

MOUNT OURAY FROM THE COCHETOPA HILLS

IV

MONARCH PASS TO COPPER MOUNTAIN

The Sawatch Range

From the minute we began the climb out of Monarch Pass, I felt like I was re-entering, if not my backyard, then at least my neck of the woods. And that felt both good and bad. I like familiarity as much as the next man, but, in some ways, it seems the closer I am to home, the harder it is to think of a trip as an adventure, with all the concomitant perils and vagaries that both connote and denote adventure. But, in a mountain range that boasts 15 fourteeners, three spectacular wilderness areas — the Collegiate Peaks, Mount Massive and Holy Cross — and some of the most intense topography in the Rockies, there is plenty of room for thrills, chills and spills, despite the fact that my humble abode lies just over the next ridge. I knew I had to resist the temptation to view this 10-day, 130-mile section from Monarch Pass to Copper Mountain Ski Area, which is located a stone's throw from my home in Breckenridge, as a mellow, downhill amble toward home and hearth simply because home and hearth are realitvely close. I silently reminded myself as we walked around the backside of Monarch Ski Area that I had to keep my focus and my concentration, lest something bad happen. There is no such thing as a mellow, downhill amble when you're interfacing very directly with the Continental Divide as it winds its way through the tallest mountains in Colorado.

Actually, I entered this part of the hike with an inexplicable feeling of foreboding. I told Gay before we parted ways at Monarch Pass that something about this expedition would be different by the time we reached Copper Mountain. I couldn't guess what, but something.

This section started out fairly inauspiciously. After spending a night in a motel in Salida, I realized that, because I had been so busy stuffing bratwursts into my mouth when we arrived at Monarch Pass, I had neglected to check out where the CDT crosses Highway 50. The night before getting back on the trail, we stayed at a Forest Service campground just below the pass. Gay and I decided to check out the trail situation so we wouldn't have to waste any time doing so the next morning. We drove back and forth on the highway near Monarch Pass several times and could see neither hide nor hair of the CDT. We stopped in the visitors' center at the pass, and I asked several of the high school-age employees about it. They all responded with the kind of blank stares that only teenagers can produce. Judging from their nonplussed expressions I may as well have just asked them to explain the tonal intricacies of the Ramah subdialect of Navaho. We were recommended to one of the few employees at the visitors' center old enough to shave, and he gave us what seemed to be pretty knowledgeable and specific directions to the trail. I'm certain he and his pimple-faced cohorts are still chuckling.

We drove slowly down the highway looking for the supposed trail before parking the car in frustration. We walked around for a full hour, following anything even remotely resembling a trail into the woods until it petered out, which it always did. If a bunny rabbit had hippity-hopped across Monarch Pass in 1863, we followed its tracks, hoping against hope it was the Continental Divide Trail. It wasn't.

Finally, we gave up. According to my map, the CDT crosses Old Monarch Pass Road, a dirt track that used to be the main connection between Salida and Gunnison. Old Monarch Pass Road turns off Highway 50 a few miles east of the visitors' center. Three miles up, we passed the CDT, replete with signs and a trailhead register. And, sure enough, a fine-looking section of trail was heading back toward Monarch. We simply could not imagine where that trail crossed Highway 50, but I was too exasperated to look any more. I told Gay that, in the morning, we would have her drive us back up here rather than spend even one more second looking for the trail out of Monarch Pass. I was relieved beyond belief that I had someone to drive me around on this trail quest. It would have been especially frustrating to be unsuccessfully looking for the CDT on foot with a heavy pack.

My frustration at this point transcended our difficult search for the CDT. Gary had opted to sit back at the campground while we went trail hunting. He did not even pretend to volunteer to assist us, and that attitude was starting to irritate me. For time number 3 million, rightly or wrongly, I felt like I was carrying the full load of this journey on my back. Truth be told, my patience with Gary was wearing thin, and my perception that Gary was just going along for the ride while Gay and I took care of everything on this hike was beginning to permeate a high percentage of my thoughts. I was starting to get bitter toward my partner. One of the unfortunate things I know about myself and that my friends know about me is that rarely do I ever regain a positive feeling for someone once the slide toward negativity has begun.

It was a fine summer morning, clear in every direction with only the slightest hint of breeze. The trail followed a series of steep snowcat roads along the boundary of Monarch Ski Area. It was

interesting to see this place in the summer, without snow. Monarch Pass averages more than 350 inches of snow a year, making it the second-snowiest part of the state, after Wolf Creek Pass. Any place that gets that much snow exists as two different season-based worlds; the Monarch Pass of summer is a different place from the Monarch Pass of winter.

Monarch is one of the last of the "little" ski areas left in Colorado. It has four double lifts, a small lodge and a low-key ambiance that used to define downhill skiing in this state. I have only skied here once, but Gay, who hails from Cañon City — only two hours away — practically grew up skiing at Monarch.

Looking down from the ridge above this anachronistic and diminutive ski area can lay one serious case of sadness on anyone who loves this state for reasons that have little or nothing to do with the prosperity that now dominates the Colorado mindset. Monarch Ski Area is like a window on Colorado's funky and rugged past. One by one, this kind of ski area is dying. Since I moved to Colorado in 1982, 10 small ski areas have gone out of business, and the mega-resorts that now dominate the ski industry have grown bigger as they have grown uglier and less personal. I am not naive about the social Darwinistic nature of business — especially the ski business. Still, I feel perfectly justified in pining hopelessly for a past in Colorado that did not pass away all that long ago. It's almost like you can still reach out and touch it, but it's long gone.

Every few hundred yards, we passed a CDT marker attached to a fine wooden post. After the previous night's trail-location fiasco at Monarch Pass, I was heartened to see some signage. Then, quite suddenly, there were markers no more, and there would not be for two full days. Just as suddenly, the tread disappeared, and we found ourselves once more following cairns as we hiked through an astounding section of tundra. Just past the ski area, the trail climbed straight up to the Divide. It was arduous and slow hiking. Below us to the east, directly beneath a precipitous and massive snow cornice, Waterdog Lakes dominated a lush valley that was as awe inspiring as any we had seen so far on the hike. (I love having my awe inspired.) Though the Sawatch Range is less isolated and much more visited than the San Juans, it is no less beautiful.

To the north lay Bald and Banana mountains, which, somehow, we needed to pass. My Trails Illustrated map had us turning east, traversing the south side of Bald Mountain before crossing its east flank, just west of Banana's summit, then descending into Hunt Lake. But, as much as I squinted and strained my eyes from a distance of less than a mile, I could not for the life of me see where a trail — even one as locationally injudicious as the CDT — could possibly go. The terrain simply looked too rugged for safe human passage. As I was concentrating on my map, all of the unexplainable and unseen forces that control the cosmos and our part in the cosmos summoned up the totality of their expressive powers and directed those powers straight to my forehead. The message was: LOOK UP NOW, NUMBSKULL!!! I did so, just in time to see Cali bounding across the mammoth cornice that dropped several hundred feet into Waterdog Lakes. She was in the process of taking one last playful bound that, if completed, would most certainly have been her last live act.

I yelled as loudly, intensely and frantically as I could, and Cali froze, midfrolic. She was less than a foot from the edge, and turned and looked at me like, "Ah, Dad, you never let me have any fun" Cali is a dog that flat-out loves snow, and I should have known she would head over to that cornice as soon as she saw it. But my focus was elsewhere. I called her over to me, wondering how I could let her know that she had just come within 12 inches of causing me a lot of grief and inconvenience. She rolled her eyes and ran off after a butterfly. Just as I had feared, I had momentarily lost my awareness, and my dog had almost perished as a result. It was only at this time and point that I realized how attached I had become to my mutt. I had rescued her from the dog pound only seven months prior, but, in that short time, she had definitely taken up residence in my heart.

I wondered if this near-dog-catastrophe was the reason for the feeling of foreboding I had had the previous night and earlier in the day.

The line of cairns continued up a calf-ripping hill that ended on a manicured section of tread that mysteriously appeared out of nowhere on the west side of Bald Mountain. Something was amiss, direction-wise. Once again, the map was saying one thing and the ground was saying another. I took my pack off and waited for Gary. When he arrived 10 minutes later, I asked to look at the Trails Illustrated map I had lent him for this section. I owned two maps of this stretch, and I had accidentally laid the more recent edition on Gary. It indicated that the trail passed along the western flank of Bald Mountain. Whew. Map reality and trail reality had just synchronized, and all was well with the orientation part of the world.

The descent into Hunt Lake was knee wracking, and that reality was exacerbated by the fact that I was toting my heaviest pack so far. In addition to carrying all the trail food I had measured and meticulously packed months ago back in Breckenridge, I had included a couple of extra treats procured at the very last minute from the Salida Safeway.

KATY AND GIGI FIELDER, SAWATCH RANGE

Those "couple of extra treats" ended up weighing at least 10 pounds. I had candy, cookies, Triscuits, some more candy and cookies, Kaiser rolls, two kinds of cheese (and I don't really even like cheese), turkey and salami. But, was I smart enough to leave behind the pre-packaged trail food that all these treats could replace, sustenance-wise? Of course not. Thus, I was carrying three or so days of redundant rations. That meant I had plenty of chow — which was good — but it also meant that I could barely make my way up the trail without swaying side to side under my load.

By the time we got down to an unnamed tarn just above Hunt Lake, we were all very ready for a break. I took Cali's pack off and let her swim in the frigid water. I was still shaken by her brush with death and the nightmarish thought of how I would have told Gay the Bad Doggy News had Cali perished up on that cornice. I vowed then and there to never, ever, under any circumstances tell her about the Almost Bad Doggy News.

As I ate some cheese and Triscuits and salami and cookies and candy, I stopped chomping long enough to study the surrounding topography. I realized I was sitting in perhaps the most scenic spot in all of Colorado. (It's amazing how much splendid territory you just blow by with scarcely a glance while on a long hike.) This was alpine territory without equal. On the other side of the tarn was a 200-foot multi-hued cliff face with a veritable multitude of gray boulders at its base. The Divide ridge, which we had just descended, was golf course green and so rock strewn we could barely make out the trail we had just followed. Down valley, treeline lay softly in wait for us, and, for one of the few times all summer, we found ourselves surrounded by wildflowers of many species and colors. I did not want to leave.

It was almost distressing to descend back into the trees, and all the more so because the CDT intersected a Jeep track near Hunt Lake. And a nasty track this was: It was so rough and rocky, it was hard to walk on. I could not imagine any vehicle making it up here, yet there were plenty of tire tracks. This sorry excuse for a vehicle-accessible thoroughfare went downhill in a big way, and our knees were soon killing us from the descent as much as our feet were killing us from impacting the rocky dirt road. Several other dirt roads branched off, and we were soon at the point of nervously making educated directional guesses. The last thing we wanted was to mess up in such a way that we had to climb back up to Hunt Lake. But we made it to Boss Lake Reservoir, which is right where we should have been. The map indicated we needed to cross the lake/reservoir's dam and head straight down to the Middle Fork of the South Arkansas River. There was a small trail right where one was supposed to be, but no sign. We gulped, crossed our fingers, hoped for the best and followed the trail. We had already lost more elevation than we had gained climbing from Monarch Pass to the side of Bald Mountain, and we were getting

SUNRISE, COLLEGIATE PEAKS WILDERNESS

more and more concerned with each downward step. The trail was ill defined, overgrown and poorly graded — meaning it must be the CDT. What else could such a trail be?

I finally came to a log bridge that crossed a small, clear creek that I assumed to be the Middle Fork. And, a few feet further on, there was a dirt road, which I assumed to be the Middle Fork Road. But there was no way to be sure. Before Gary caught up with me, I thought I heard some people talking. I dropped my pack and walked down the road. Sure enough, there were a couple of good ol' boys just standing next to their Jeeps, sipping beer and shooting the breeze. When they confirmed my location, I was tempted to kiss them heartily on the lips, but it just didn't seem like an appropriate thing to do.

By the time I got back to my pack, Gary was sitting there, waiting and smoking his pipe. Now, having the cigar habit I have, I cannot in good conscience make any observation save the most casual about someone smoking. But I have never known any non-cigarette smoker (which are a whole different breed) to puff as much as Gary. I only pull out my stogies in camp. Gary lights up his pipe every time he stops for a break on the trail. He stops to smack a mosquito or check out his map, he lights up. It's hilarious. For the rest of my life, every mental image I retain of Gary will include that blasted pipe stuck between his incisors.

According to the map, the rest of our day's itinerary would be the proverbial piece of cake. That is always a bad sign. The plan was to hike up the Middle Fork Road for a few more miles before looking for the nirvana-like campsite that certainly awaited us. We figured to hike 10, maybe 11 miles today. This road was in a lot better shape than the beast we had followed from Hunt Lake to Boss Lake Reservoir. It actually made for some pretty pleasant walking. After a mile, we once again crossed the Middle Fork — something that ran contrary to the map. But, heck, we figured that such a deviation was small taters compared to any of 100 map/reality deviations we had already experienced. But, soon, the heretofore pleasant dirt road deteriorated substantially. We were having to negotiate massive mud bogs and climb over blown-down trees every 50 feet. This road just plain smelled wrong. We were, however, definitely heading up the right valley, and that provided a modicum of consolation. After climbing over our 499th and 500th blowdown, we decided, being the Daniel Boones we were, something was sorely amiss. I told Gary that, at the first clearing, I would bushwhack up the side of the Divide ridge at the base of Clover Mountain to see if I could catch a glimpse of the correct route that surely existed somewhere in this valley. We were both fairly convinced the right road had to be on the other side of the Middle Fork.

Before we reached a suitable place for my bushwhack, though, Gary noticed something shiny in the woods to the east. He had just eyeballed the gleaming roofs

MOUNT YALE (14,196')

85

MOUNT YALE REFLECTS ON LAKE REBECCA (BOTH PHOTOGRAPHS)

Huron Peak (14,005')

of two cabins. We hacked our way through the undergrowth and crossed the Middle Fork and, lo and behold, there was the dirt road we should have been following all along. How we ended up on the wrong side of the river on the wrong road I will never know. What I did know was that these two cabins were terrific, and they were open for public use — just like the cabin we stayed in near Marshall Pass. Gary took one, and I took the other.

There was yard furniture, an outhouse, a nice stock of firewood and a pretty little creek passing a few feet from "my" cabin. As I have said, musty old cabins are not my favorite places to sleep out in the woods, but these were superlative digs, well tended and airy. Cali was wagging her tail so hard, I thought she was going to take off rump first like a helicopter.

Inside, each of the cabins had a table, a couple of primitive bunks with mattresses, a woodstove, several chairs, books, basic dishes and a little canned food. Cozy trailside accommodations indeed.

I sidled over to the creek, which flowed down from the flanks of Mount Aetna, for a wash. The water was crystal clear and, unfortunately, was so cold that I almost went into convulsions just walking in ankle deep. The second I had completely declothed, a huge gunrack-bearing Ford truck drove by. I was within 50 feet of the road, but had mistakenly thought that I was far off enough in the boonies that I could bathe in solitude. I sheepishly hid my nakedness behind a T-shirt and

ALONG THE TRAIL, TEXAS CREEK

innocently smiled and waved as the vehicle passed, its burly, tattooed passenger and her husband laughing heartily. When the truck was out of sight, I returned to the business of trying to get at least moderately unskinky when yet another truck passed. Shortly thereafter, two ATVers drove by, then two more trucks. Almost certainly, later tonight, an entire country/western bar down in Garfield or Salida will be filled with people exchanging observations about the strange man who was standing ankle-deep and naked in the little stream up by the cabins on the Middle Fork.

After changing into my camp clothes, I laid out a dinner spread on the table outside. I had so much store-bought fresh food, it looked like I was having a one-man medieval banquet. All I needed was a lute player and a court jester to complete the scene. A civilized (to say nothing of pack-lightening) feast seemed appropriate in such a civilized setting. I gorged myself to the point that, had an amoeba made its way down my

THE THREE APOSTLES

MAKING TIME ON THE DIVIDE

gullet, my stomach would have exploded. Then I had a half dozen cookies for dessert.

By the time the sun set behind the Divide, I waddled back to my cabin. From my food bag I pulled the backpacking-food dinner that I would have eaten tonight were it not for the fact

that I was carrying an entire Safeway store in my pack. I placed that food on the shelf next to the canned food that was already here — my donation to the cabin's survival rations, as well as to the John Fayhee Backpack-Lightening Crusade.

We would pass the 300-mile mark tomorrow, and already I was getting tired of my trail dinners. As we all know, good diet plays an important role in any successful athletic undertaking. Thus, my trail dinners consisted of such tantalizingly wholesome staples as whole wheat, miso-flavored ramen; home-dried broccoli, carrots, mushrooms and zucchini; freeze-dried chicken; all-natural bullion; instant brown rice; dried beans; spices; soy sauce and ample quantities of Mongolian Fire Oil. That's the kind of chow that fuels a long self-propelled journey. It's also the kind of chow that gets enthusiastically left on a cabin shelf when there is a tastier, though less healthy, alternative.

Before hitting the hay, I noticed there was a logbook in the cabin, and I opted to read it rather than one of my books. (I was carrying two for this stretch: Larry McMurtry's *Dead Man's Walk* — which was so repulsively odious I threw it away at my earliest opportunity — and e.e. cummings' *100 Selected Poems*.) Logbooks can either make for some captivating reading, or they can bore you to tears instantly. Most times, it's a mix of the two. A single logbook, whether it is found atop a peak or in a cabin or hut, will usually be a haphazard mix of "We're the Schmo family from Lubbock! There are four of us! We climbed a mountain! What a glorious day! We sure are looking forward to eating pizza tonight!" and 37 straight pages of unindented, single-spaced text penned by someone who fervently believes he or she was Thoreau in a past life.

JOHN FAYHEE CONSUMES HIS MORNING COFFEE
GAY GANGEL-FAYHEE

This logbook contained a very amusing tête-à-tête between two people who are apparently regulars at these cabins. One was a snowmobiler and virulent anti-cross-country skier, the other was a cross-country skier and virulent anti-snowmobiler. There were exchanges like, "You blankety-blank self-propelled elitists would all die if there weren't snowmobilers to come in and rescue you when you get hurt!" and "You blankety-blank fat snowmobilers and your blankety-blank stink sleds pollute the entire planet with noxious emissions and we hope you all drive off a cliff!" There were several rounds of these kinds of

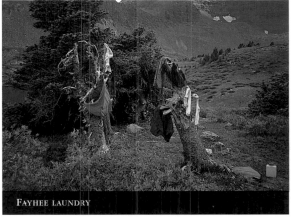
FAYHEE LAUNDRY
GAY GANGEL-FAYHEE

TRURO PEAK, COLLEGIATE PEAKS WILDERNESS

ALPINE GARDEN BELOW THE CONTINENTAL DIVIDE, WHITE RIVER NATIONAL FOREST

TARN, WHITE RIVER NATIONAL FOREST

ON THE DIVIDE ABOVE INDEPENDENCE PASS

HIKING THROUGH THE GARDEN

exchanges, which covered several visits by each writer spanning most of a year. By the end of the logbook, there was an exchange of addresses and telephone numbers, with entries like, 'You're too scared to call me, and, if you do, I will kick your butt all the way up the side of the mountain!'

It was hilarious. I wondered what would happen if the two children in question ever showed up here at the same time. Probably nothing, for, as I well know, it's easy to talk big behind the anonymity and relative safety of a pen and paper.

There was a more somber entry in this logbook. Two winters before, a couple of college kids from Colorado State University had been staying here in the dead of winter. They had left with their two dogs before dawn to attempt to summit one of the surrounding peaks. They got whacked full tilt by an avalanche. Both humans lived; both dogs died, with their remains unrecovered. Some of the ink had run, like tears had fallen on the page as the story was penned. I can just imagine how this poor kid felt — the winter winds blowing chilly and cold outside this snug little cabin. Every time the wind howled, he probably wondered if it was one of his dogs, calling for his master to come and rescue him and take him home. This tale

of woe ended with an admonition that, if anyone ever finds the dogs' collars, they be sent to this address.

I looked down at Cali, who might well have met her demise this morning. She was sleeping, very contentedly.

Before leaving the next morning, I took a stroll to the close-at-hand outhouse. Inside was a copy of the *Summit Daily News*, which I helped start in 1989. I don't know whether finding a paper that was once such a large part of my life in such a venue was a compliment or an insult. But, since there was no toilet paper, I took it as a compliment.

Two miles past the cabins, the road terminated, and, shortly thereafter, the trail fizzled out in the middle of an endless sea of willows.

I hate willows.

First, understand that, when we talk of willows in Colorado, we are not talking about anything "weeping," unless it is the person having to walk through them. Tundra willows are anywhere from knee to head high, and they are particularly notorious for attacking passing hikers. They are adept at grabbing exposed legs and working feverishly at scratching as much flesh as possible in as short a time as possible. This is made all the more irksome by the fact that,

JOHN FAYHEE CHECKING IN AT THE TRAILHEAD

GAY GANGEL-FAYHEE

early in the morning, when they are dew soaked, willows have a way of mystically funneling quantities of water that exceed their weight ten-fold directly into one's socks. You pass through a willow grove before the morning dew has evaporated, and you are assured of discomfort for many miles to come.

Certainly, I value willows for environmental reasons. I once heard them described as the "mangroves of the mountains," meaning, I guess, that they are very valuable because they provide protection from predators for nesting birds and small mammals. Therefore, it would be considered tacky for a card-carrying environmentalist such as myself to carry a backpackable weed-whacker for the express purpose of obliterating every willow I come across.

When at long last I broke out into the tundra proper, I was soaked through and wondering if there were such a thing as freeze-dried herbicides and defoliants. My spirits were raised, though, by the tremendous tundra leading up to Chalk Creek Pass. I had left the cabins before Gary was even packed, so I parked it at the top of the pass to wait for him. I figured it would be at least an hour, as Gary seemed loathe to leave the comfort of those cabins behind. He looked like he could joyously hang out there for many consecutive months. He even said that, after this hike is over, he might return to the cabins for a couple of weeks. Lovely though they were, I could not imagine a person wanting to stay there for more than a night or two. But, that's the difference between Gary and me. He was a Pueblo Indian in a previous life; I was a Sahara-dwelling nomadic Tuareg.

I parked on the alpine grass and lay back on my pack. I pulled out a couple tons of Triscuits and salami and had myself a nice post-breakfast, pre-mid-morning-snack snack.

SUNSET AT LINKINS LAKE, HUNTER-FRYINGPAN WILDERNESS

Fifteen minutes later, I picked Gary out way down below, making his way through those abominable willows. It would take him at least 45 minutes to reach the pass. In the meantime, I was perfectly happy to sit up here above the clouds, admiring the miniature tundra flowers dotting the landscape. Every spring, I promise myself this will be the year I try to learn the names of the lovely and delicate flowers that dwell in the tundra. Every year, I fail to do so. After 14 years of calling Colorado home, I still only know the names of a few flower species, and sometimes that is a touch embarrassing, as people assume that, because I am an outdoor writer, I must be part naturalist. I long ago gave up trying to rationalize my ignorance about wildflower nomenclature. I used to say things like, "I may not know the name, but I know the flower," and hope that was enough of a smokescreen that anyone unfortunate enough to have that drivel laid on them would not realize how silly both the statement and the sentiment were until I was long gone.

I have also tried arguing that I was simply incapable of learning the names of wildflowers — that "I don't think that way"— but that, too, was a smokescreen. When I was working as a land surveyor back in Virginia, I learned, out of necessity, the names of at least 100 kinds of trees.

I have no excuses for my flower ignorance, save laziness. A couple nights ago, Gary expressed aloud his wonder at my love for the tundra. He told me that, while he considers it beautiful and all (I mean, who could not?), he preferred the Krummholz zone, the point where the mountainside bids adios to the trees. My ponderous, Walt Whitman-like response was, "Uh, I dunno, I just like it."

For many years, I have attempted to define objectively for people like my wife, as well as myself, why I love the tundra so much. I don't believe it's the lack of trees because, first, I don't have anything against trees (I actually like trees very much, as long as they don't block too many of my views), and, second, well, central Kansas lacks trees, and I

MARSH MARIGOLD ALONG LOST MAN CREEK

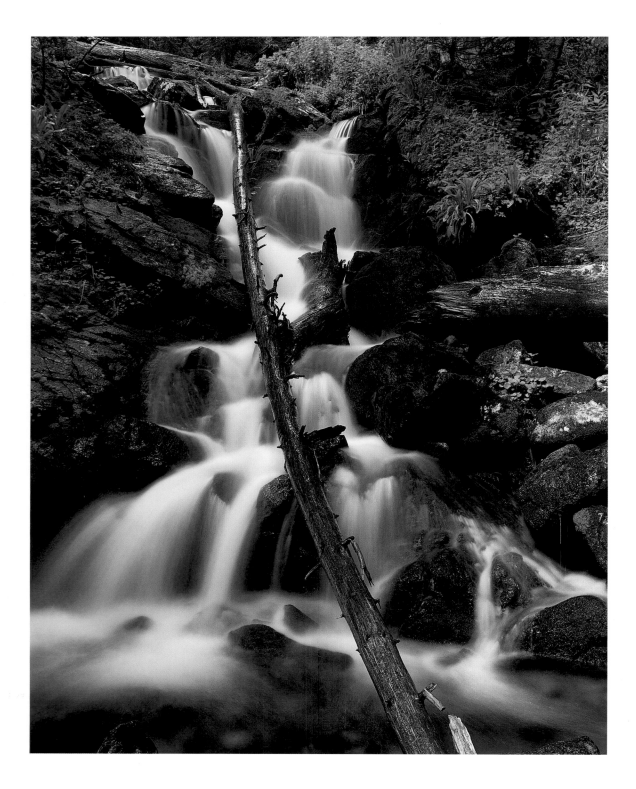

don't exactly feel any sense of attachment to the heart of the Sunflower State.

I am the least spiritual person I have ever met, and I am very happy about that reality. I am blessed in that never, ever, ever do I waste time contemplating the "big questions" — the variations on the Why Are We Here? and Where Are We Going? themes — that grab the attention and often absorb so many otherwise intelligent folks. But, I have hobnobbed with enough people about these kinds of matters to know that the closest I come to not being spiritual antimatter is when I am in the tundra.

I long ago concluded that I am flat-out unable to define my love for this environment objectively, except in symptomatic ways. I think tundra wildflowers are the most beautiful things on Earth — even more beautiful than coral reefs, and, yes, even more beautiful than women. I love the red and green lichen-infested rock fields, and the sense of fear when heavy weather moves in, and the clean crispness of the air, and the views that span entire time zones. Every time I ascend into the tundra, I get goose bumps. Every single time.

When I'm laying there in the thick grass at 13,000 feet getting scorched by the intense alpine sun, a feeling comes over me that is beyond objective description. I feel simultaneously tranquil and energized, both meditative and lucid. I feel bonded with this celestial object we call Mother Earth in a way that I have experienced in no other place or kind of place.

This is the place I am most at peace.

The tundra is also a great place to smoke cigars and read.

I was once corrected by someone who obviously needed to get a life fast when I used the term "tundra" while speaking about above-treeline territory in Colorado. This person had a PhD in advanced molecular snobbery, and he had that academician-type way of rolling his eyes so far upward when he felt he was in the presence of an intellectual inferior who was muttering something he considered inane and/or banal that it seemed like his view-pods could easily rotate 180 degrees in his head and return to the front-and-center from the bottom of his eye sockets. He told me in no uncertain terms that tundra per se (whenever an educated person uses "per se" in casual conversation, you know you're in argumentative trouble) was a sub-arctic phenomenon only. Colorado, I was told, had no tundra, because it is not bionomically sub-arctic. Then what, I asked, should we call all this treeless territory up here in our mountains? "Areas that are similar to tundra, but not tundra," he replied, in a superior-sounding tone of voice that made me want to whack him with my hiking staff.

LINKINS LAKE

STORM, MOUNT MASSIVE WILDERNESS

Once more, I was very relieved that I have managed to steer pretty much clear of all things even remotely academic throughout my life.

Turns out, though, that the man was wrong as wrong gets. What we have in Colorado is "alpine tundra," as opposed to "sub-arctic tundra," but, basically, if it walks like a duck and quacks like a duck, it's tundra. Whether in Siberia, Alaska or Colorado, tundra boasts pretty much the same flower species and, often, the same wildlife, though I'm pretty sure Colorado is musk-ox free, which is a shame. It's climate and topography (no trees and plenty of snow and mud) that define tundra. What Alaska and Siberia gain climatically from latitude, we gain from altitude.

I thought Gary would be in a foul mood after dealing with the willows on his way up, but he was in good spirits, and we were soon on our way, descending into Hancock Lake, which is connected by dirt road to the ghost town of Hancock and the almost-ghost town of St. Elmo. We had to walk down that road, and I told Gary that, if there was anyone driving out, I was going to bum a ride. Though the new insoles I bought in Salida were working wonderfully, my feet were still getting tired of road walking. Gary concurred with enthusiasm. Alas, it was not to be; though there were cars at Hancock Lake, they were all owned by people who had no intention of leaving their fishing spots for several hours.

It was 2 miles down to the Hancock town site. From there, we began what a sign billed as a 3.5-mile ascent to the "Old Alpine Tunnel"— through which, back in days of yore, trains used to pass beneath the Divide. It was a mellow railroad grade, and I made it in 45 minutes, which meant it was not 3.5 miles, as I have never hiked 3.5 miles uphill with a full pack in 45 minutes in my life. At the site of the tunnel, which either collapsed or was collapsed long ago, there were two great trails to choose from. One switchbacked steeply up to the Divide ridge, while the other — which was not on the map — made its way more or less in the direction we needed to go down into a lovely creek bottom. We opted to take the latter trail, mainly, I guess, because it was heading downhill. We descended into a lush valley, and, as soon as we found ourselves in the middle of another endless sea of willows, the trail just disappeared. We figured we must have lost the trail, that it must be around here "somewhere," as it was too good simply to end in the middle of a willow thicket. We spent the next two hours looking for it and ended up bushwhacking through the largest expanse of willows on earth. By the time we intersected the trail we should have taken from the tunnel site to the top of the

Divide in the first place, we were talking about starting a group called something like Citizens Wholeheartedly and Enthusiastically United Against Willows and All That Willows Stand For Forevermore.

Once again, the trail on the map went one way and the trail on the ground went another. The trail was good for about a mile, until it topped out at 12,300 feet on a small saddle that crossed a spur ridge. From there until the long drop into the North Fork of Chalk Creek, we followed cairns over bumpy tundra.

By the time we reached Chalk Creek, we had gone 14 miles, and that was enough for a day defined by bushwhacking through willows. After camp chores were done and our respective smokes were lit, we talked about our upcoming itinerary. We had a mini-food drop planned in Twin Lakes four days hence, and I told Gary I thought we had plenty of hard hiking between here and there. I could see his mental gears churning.

"What do you mean, four more days to Twin Lakes? It's only three more days."

"No, Gary, it's four more days."

He had misread his itinerary, and, therefore, was one day short on food and fuel. He had left a lot of food back at the cabins, and now was staring down some short rations. I had, likewise, left some food back at the cabins, and, since I had been eating like crazy for two days to lighten my pack, I did not have a ton of extra chow either. We pulled out our food bags and inventoried our joint supplies. Gary seemed convinced that he would not die of starvation between here and Twin Lakes. He was going to have to cut back on his in-camp hot chocolate from 300 cups a day to only 275, but he thought he could limp through all right. His biggest concern was fuel. Gary measures his fuel very carefully before each stretch, making certain that he does not carry so much as an extra milligram. He said he might have to bum some fuel off me.

Gary's fuel problem was solved early the next morning as we were walking up the Tincup Pass Road. I spied a pickup truck with a camper shell parked back in the woods, and I asked the owner if he had any extra Coleman fuel to spare. He did, and he very kindly topped off Gary's bottle.

The next few days blurred by. We were in the middle third of our hike, which is always strange from a motivational perspective. We've been on the trail a long time (30 days out of Cumbres), but Wyoming is still a long way off. We can see light at neither end of the tunnel. At this stage of any long trek, you find yourself sort of just going through the motions — getting up in the morning, breaking camp, hiking all day, setting up camp, going to bed — even though those motions might be taking place in the middle of some beautiful territory. We blew past Mirror Lake, across Cottonwood Pass and Texas Creek roads, along the Timberline Trail up and over the Divide on the newly constructed Gunnison Spur of the Colorado Trail, down into the Collegiate Peaks Wilderness, past the wonderfully preserved ghost town of Winfield, and, finally, back onto the Colorado Trail proper just south of Hope Pass.

There was more going on here, though, than the middle-third-of-a-long-hike syndrome. It was getting to the point that Gary and I were hardly even talking to each other, and, when we did converse, it was either straightforward, logistical trail talk or snipping. We weren't even pretending to try to get along. There were several days when we only saw each other a couple of times. We were setting up our tents farther and farther away from each other at camp. I did not desire to continue under these social circumstances. I had realized as far back as the La Garitas that the civilization-based, real-life tension that was knotting me up before I left on this hike was long gone. But in its place was a tension of a whole different color. It was based on the fact that, when I got right down to it, I really didn't like Gary, and it was equally obvious that he didn't like me. Our values, morals, ethics, perspectives, demeanors, manners and mannerisms were like night and day, and that was wearing on both of us. I could scarcely think about anything save how I wanted to

SUNRISE AT NOTCH LAKE, MOUNT MASSIVE WILDERNESS

dump Gary. But, since I had never had a hiking partner before, I did not know how to go about broaching the subject.

The climb up Hope Pass is a killer. From Clear Creek Road, where we camped, it's 3,000 vertical feet and two miles to the top. With a foodless pack I made it in 45 minutes. I was flying. Behind me, I saw Gary far below. In front, I could see the Tenmile Range — the western boundary of Summit County, and one of the mountain ranges I can see from my yard.

I did not wait for Gary; I had no desire to wait. I flew some more, and arrived at a small parking area on Highway 82 by 11:00. I had gone 13 miles in three hours. My friend Currie Craven, who was bringing our food drop, wasn't scheduled to arrive until 1:00, so I de-packed and found a shady spot next to a creek. Gary arrived at 12:30 and immediately went downstream to find his own spot. We didn't exchange two words. When Currie arrived, I had to go find Gary.

Currie drove us to Lakeview Campground, and, even though the tension between Gary and I was knife-cutting thick, we had a great time. Currie had brought with him more food than any 20 hikers could have consumed in one afternoon and evening. But we put a good-sized dent in his provisions. Currie and I took an after-dinner walk around the campground, and I told him that, when we arrived at Copper Mountain, I was going to give Gary the ol' heave ho from this hike. Currie observed that it didn't seem like Gary and I were on the same page. I was tempted to lay the news on Gary right then and there, sending him back to Summit County with Currie, but that would have been very unfair to Currie, whom I count as one of my dearest compadres. I decided that I could last four more days.

I was wrong.

At Rock Creek, an easy 14 miles along a well-coiffed section of the Colorado Trail from Twin Lakes, I decided this could go on no longer. Just before bed, I had asked Gary to start taking better care of my maps, and he essentially blew me off. As I was making my way along the perfectly manicured trail the next morning, I was fuming. I stopped at the Turquoise Lake Road, just outside of Leadville, and removed my back, waiting for Gary. When he caught up, I chickened out. I simply did not know how to word what clearly needed to be worded. It was especially troublesome because I understood on all levels that I had certainly played my part in all this. I am not the easiest person to get along with. My point was not that there was anything wrong with Gary or, for that matter, that there was anything wrong with me. We were just so different that any attempts to continue this on-trail

relationship would be totally artificial. I did not want to spend the last 300 miles of this hike waiting for the hike to get over and done with just so I could part ways with Gary.

I told him that my back was acting up — which it was — and that, since I had already hiked the last 17 miles between Turquoise Lake and Copper Mountain when I hiked the Colorado Trail, I'd just as soon hitchhike into Leadville, call Gay and have her come pick us up. I told Gary I could use the extra two days rest. I couldn't believe I was being such a wuss. We got a ride into town easily enough. After a meal in the Leadville Diner, we walked to a local convenience store and I called Gay.

"Oh dear," was all she could say.

While we were sitting in the convenience store parking lot waiting for Gay, I told Gary that, for reasons I could not fathom, I was having a terrible time on this hike. I told him that, because long-distance hiking is my favorite pastime, if I'm not having fun, then something is clearly wrong between my ears. I told him that, therefore, I needed to continue this hike by myself, so I could figure all this out, and I hoped he understood. I spent the next 15 minutes aggressively shouldering every bit of the blame for our failed relationship, and Gary spent those 15 minutes agreeing with me on every count.

Gay drove us home, we went out to dinner that night in Breckenridge and, the next morning, Gary was gone.

WINTER NEAR HAGERMAN PASS, SAN ISABEL NATIONAL FOREST

To where, I do not know. Maybe back down to those little cabins near Monarch Pass. Maybe back to Michigan. He talked a little bit about continuing the hike on his own, but it was obvious to Gay and me that he had become too accustomed to the logistical support that Gay and my friends were providing on this hike. There was no way he was going to pull it off on his own. To this day, I have heard nary a syllable from Gary, and I doubt I ever will.

I took a day off, and, the day after that, my friend Mark Fox drove me back around to the trail, and Cali and I dayhiked from Camp Hale over Elk Ridge to Copper Mountain. For the past 400 miles, I had expected to feel exhilarated when I arrived at Copper. Now all I felt was deflated and guilty for dumping Gary. I know I should not feel this way, as trail life presents a rough venue for developing and maintaining any relationship. Gay and I have had some of our worst fights on the trail. I felt culpable nonetheless, and that guilt would not quickly go away. But, mixed in with a whole mental grab bag of "what-if?" and "where did I go wrong?"-type contemplations, was an overwhelming feeling of relief, like I had just come up for air for the first time since Cumbres Pass.

I took off three full days in Breckenridge, during which time I barely left the house. I set the world record for HBO-watching, and I ate constantly. Gradually, I started to get my good spirit back and, when I hit the trail again at Copper Mountain, there was fire burning in my soul. I felt wonderful.

As I was packing, I remembered I had told Gay back at Monarch Pass that something would be different about this hike when I reached Copper Mountain. I was thank-God-fully right.

POND, HAGERMAN PASS

HOMESTAKE PEAK, HOLY CROSS WILDERNESS

SKIING TO HOMESTAKE PEAK

V

COPPER MOUNTAIN TO BERTHOUD PASS

Over to the Front Range

The Summit County section underscores the difficulty of designing and building a 3,100-mile trail from Mexico to Canada. In 1994, the U.S. Forest Service finished its Environmental Impact Statement (EIS) for the CDT through Colorado. Though it was a tedious, multi-year process, the completion of that document was reasonably straightforward — except for the section from Copper Mountain to Rollins Pass and one stretch in the far northern part of the state. Those two sections were removed from the statewide EIS because, basically, no one could agree on where the CDT ought to go. There were problems with mining claims, endangered species and private property, as well as a fair amount of administrative disorganization on the part of the Forest Service. By 1997, the route through Summit County had still not been determined, so Gay (who joined me for the 83-mile hike to Grand Lake via Berthoud Pass) and I opted to reconnect with the Divide right out of the Eisenhower Tunnel, at which point I-70 travels beneath the mountains for 2 miles. My long-time Tae Kwon Do instructor, Rob Lee, drove us up to the tunnel and opted to walk with us for a few miles. I had never hiked here before and had my fingers crossed that the trail marked on the map actually existed. It did. Barely. For a short while. By the time we topped out on the Divide, we were following an old Jeep road from, seemingly, back before Jeeps were invented. At the point where the "road" fizzled out, Rob intelligently decided to bid us adieu.

The map indicated that we should stay atop the Divide until we approached the south flank of Hagar Mountain — one of the meanest, nastiest and gnarliest-looking peaks in this part of the state, at least from the perspective of someone who has his wife with him.

We were both nervous about taking this route, but we figured it would cut out almost a full day of hiking over Ptarmigan Pass from Silverthorne. That's a trail we've taken before, so we wanted to check out some new territory. We just hoped we wouldn't regret the decision, which meant, of course, that just because we were concerned about the possibility of regretting the decision, we would surely regret the decision. I-70 loomed obscenely below us. But, it was possible to overlook the blight of the Eisenhower Tunnel because overall the views were the best of the entire hike. I could not remember ever seeing so much of Colorado in one fell visual swoop. The sky was perfectly clear, and it seemed like we could see all the way to the Pacific. The entire northern half of the Sawatch Range opened up before us, as well as four nearby fourteeners — Evans, Bierstadt, Grays and Torreys.

Soon, we were out of sight of the tunnel, and the surrounding tundra was terrific. Then we started to cross the top end of Loveland Ski Area. There are few things on the face of the earth less attractive than ski areas in the summer. It's like seeing a beautiful actress backstage without her makeup. With lift towers and dirty parking lots and tacky structures, ski areas are plenty ugly in the winter, but, in the summer, they are beneath aesthetic contempt. Nothing but brown grass, dust and an air of neglect and tackiness. For reasons that have always escaped me, ski areas seem to be relatively free from the kind of environmentalist scrutiny that justifiably dogs the extractive industries, like mining, ranching and timbering, every minute of every day. My wife once described a ski run as the most absolute form of clear-cutting. Yet, because skiing is a healthy, outdoorsy activity where all the children sport broad smiles and rosy cheeks in glossy magazine advertisements, whatever attention environmentalists and environmental groups pay it focuses firmly on symptoms, like the expansion of an individual bowl or the cutting of a new run. They never go after the ski area jugular, trying to put the entire industry out of business, as they do with ranching, timbering and mining. Seems like the ski industry is an environmental-issue emperor with no clothes, and yet another sacred cow continues to wander through our mountains without challenge.

Once we passed Loveland, we were faced with a wide expanse of treadless tundra with no cairns. I heard Gay sigh. Her ankles still hadn't healed all the way from her tundra-hopping back in the South San Juans. I said something brilliant like, "Oh, look, honey, lucky are we — a wide expanse of treadless tundra with no cairns!" But my feigned enthusiasm does not seem to enthuse my bride. Wonder why?

Even with Gay's binoculars, I could not see where we would bail out before Hagar Mountain. Suddenly, a couple of cairns appeared on the west side of the ridge, but they must have been somebody's idea of a very bad joke. They took us down along a talus slope the size of Texas. That was the good part. The bad part was that the sideslope was, like, 70 degrees. We were hiking with our right feet up near our ears and our left feet down in the valley below, and our footing was so bad we slipped, skidded and stumbled every step.

After 45 minutes of this abject misery, we arrived at a little side ridge that actually had a reasonable trail. Soon after, we intersected with the South Fork Trail and were descending into lovely Bobtail Valley. This beautiful place almost made the final cut when the last Colorado

Bristlecone pines below Mount Bross (14,172'), Pike National Forest (both photographs)

Wilderness Act passed into law in 1993. That act established the Ptarmigan Peak Wilderness, on the west side of the close-at-hand Williams Fork Mountains. But Bobtail Valley was lopped off at the very last minute because of opposition from the Denver Water Board, which argued that the nearby Henderson Molybdenum Mine destroyed any wilderness values this valley might have. In other words, they have their eyes on the ample water found hereabouts. This area now is classified as a "Roadless Area" (meaning mountain bikes may enter, but motor vehicles may not), and I guess that's better than nothing.

By 1:00, after about 10 miles, we found one of the most bucolic campsites we had ever seen. It was a tad close to the trail, but this was a little-visited place, so we predicted absolute privacy. The sun was tweeting and the birds were shining, and we took a leisurely bath down at the creek. As soon as we were back in camp, a middle-age couple passed by. They had driven to the Jones Pass road — which we would ascend the next day — and had spent the day hiking along Bobtail Creek. I was bummed to see anyone back here, but they were very nice people and we had a pleasant chat. They lived someplace awful in the East, but the man told me he had hiked up Bobtail Creek 30 years ago, and this was his first time back.

A few minutes later, up walks a man leading three llamas. This was Kevin from California, and I had been following him all summer. As far as I knew, there were only four of us hiking the Colorado section of the Divide Trail this summer. There was one couple that started the first of June, and Kevin, who started three weeks before I did. That's one of the strange aspects of hiking a long trail — because of trail registers, you know who's ahead, but they have no idea who's behind.

Kevin camped close by, and Cali was more than a little intrigued by the llamas. Even though we were only one day out of Breckenridge, we were very envious of Kevin's provisions. With three llamas for one man, this guy was traveling comfortably and eating well. His tent was twice as large as ours, and he talked about all the books he was carrying. He had a cellular phone and maybe even a laptop computer. He seemed to not be scrimping on his chow, either. Though we weren't close enough to his camp to see what he actually ate, we suspected he was not rationing grams of peanut butter the way we were. I think I might have even smelled steak.

Before we left Cumbres Pass, there were two days on my itinerary that, above and beyond all others, had me concerned. In only two places did the words "trail undefined" appear on my maps. Considering that, for most of the way, the CDT had been the very definition of "undefined" — without being so designated on the maps — my imagination had been running amok for the past 400-plus miles. What could be so nasty that the Trails Illustrated people felt compelled to place the words "trail undefined" on their Winter Park/Central City/Rollins Pass map, which covers this section? I mean, they didn't place those words on the stretch between Stony Pass and Pole Creek, and it would be physically impossible for a trail to be any less defined than there.

AUTUMN ALONG BOREAS PASS, PIKE NATIONAL FOREST

Mount Guyot

Grays (14,270') and Torreys (14,267') peaks

This was the first of those two undefined days. I simply did not know what to expect, but, after hours of map scrutiny, I did not expect to be whistling while I walked. The morning commenced with a 2,000-foot ascent of the dirt road to Jones Pass. Since Gay had not backpacked in six weeks, she was moving slowly, and it took more than two hours to gain the Divide. From there, we knew the fun was set to begin. Though the map showed a trail from Jones Pass around to Vasquez Peak, it looked like the kind of trail that might be a little lacking in physical reality. Turned out there was no trail, and this section of the Divide was rough. We had to cross numerous stretches of steep, crumbly rock, and, all the while, Vasquez Peak was looming on the northern horizon like a bad dream. Though it's only 12,947 feet high, it looked forbidding. I had mentioned to Gay several times that we had to cross Vasquez, but she thought it must be some as-yet-unseen peak. When she realized that was Vasquez sinisterly dominating the far side of Clear Creek Valley, she gulped. I assured her that there must be some easy way up that we simply could not see from "this angle."

After climbing into and out of two deep, rock-strewn notches in the ridge, we came nose to nose with the side of Vasquez Peak. I could not believe how steep it was. Within minutes, I was walking 50 paces, stopping for a count of 50, then walking 50 more paces, with my Achilles' tendons whining the whole way. I did not even want to think about the effect this was having on Gay on her second day out. It took an hour to reach a cairn just below the summit. I took my pack off and ran with Cali to the top. By the time I returned, Gay had caught up. She was tired, but was holding up very well. I was proud of her.

Our problem now was water. This ridge was bone dry, and, according to the map, the "trail" (this being the exact spot where it is "undefined") dropped off into the headwaters of Vasquez Creek. We were in the mood both to find a campsite and slake our thirst, so going down sounded good. On the east haunch of Vasquez Peak, the whole Vasquez Creek drainage opened up, with views all the way into Middle Park. It was awesome. As I waited for Gay, I noticed we could pick our way down into the valley without following the ridge any further, which the map indicated we were supposed to do. The notion of taking a shortcut began to take hold. Gay rolled her eyes when I pitched the idea to her, but, nonetheless, she agreed. It was a mellow 1,000-foot descent, and, before long, we came across a lame excuse for a trail, which, in our fatigue, we assumed must be "the" trail. You know, "the" trail that we haven't been on for the past four hours, because there is no trail.

We were so happy about finding "the" trail that we followed it for 30 minutes, despite the fact that it was obviously heading in the completely wrong direction. "Don't worry," I assured Gay, "it's bound to wind around to the other side of the valley."

It didn't, and we ended up bushwhacking for an hour through briars and brambles and, yes, millions of willows. When we finally arrived at the east side of the valley, I felt like I had walked 200 miles since lunch. My legs weighed a ton each, like someone had poured concrete into my hiking boots and put boulders in my backpack.

Our campsite ended up being nice, even though we had to walk through willows to get to water. Before bed, I ambled up to the far side of the valley, hoping to find a trail. I did not, and we dozed off having no earthly idea what lay in store for us, trail-wise, the next day.

I awoke at first light and looked outside. I have never witnessed such a glorious sight. The alpenglow on the Divide was as deep, vibrant and rich as any I had ever seen. I quickly roused Gay and told her to get her lazy old bones out there to take some pictures. She was so drowsy and disoriented, she actually complied, while I lay there in my cozy sleeping bag, admiring the view, which faded within minutes.

I knew we were only a few miles from Berthoud Pass, but, the way things were going, I still wanted to be on the trail early, as a preemptive strike against any potential time-consuming mishaps. As difficult as this trail has been so far, I would not have been surprised if I bedded down that very night in China. Actually, I made a for once correct directional guess and we soon found ourselves following a line of diminutive cairns all the way to Vasquez Pass. From there, it's a captivating hump to the summit of Stanley Mountain, where we came across some fairly nice tread.

It stayed level and easy until we began our descent into Berthoud Pass, where my friend Patrick Brower was due to bring us a food drop. As we were making our way down to the pass, it dawned on me how much I had thoroughly enjoyed the past few days. They were difficult and stimulating, which is exactly what the Continental Divide Trail ought to be. Since the establishment of the CDT now has more momentum and corporate and governmental financial backing than ever before, I suspect the days of this trail remaining primitive and challenging are nearly gone. Colorado right now is in a monument-building mode predicated by the state's continued strong economy. My guess is, the CDT will soon become one of our more prominent monuments. In 20 years, it will be coiffed, perfumed and dressed to the nines. There will be end-to-end manicured tread, signs planted ad nauseum and very little in the way of mystery. Sure, there are a lot of stretches on this trail — especially those that follow Jeep tracks — that I would like to see improved. But, overall, I am glad I did this hike when I did, before the trailhead signs are adorned with corporate sponsorship logos.

The weather starts turning nasty as we cross busy Highway 40. We set up our tent behind the long-closed Berthoud Ski Area lodge. It's cold and wet with a hint of snow. Fall is coming to the land of thin air, and it's coming fast. That is fine by me, as fall is my favorite season.

PETTINGELL PEAK, ARAPAHO NATIONAL FOREST

Tundra pools, Vasquez Peak Wilderness (both photographs)

VI

BERTHOUD PASS TO MUDDY PASS

The Front Range

Our night behind the lodge at Berthoud Pass Ski Area was not exactly relaxing. Since U.S. Highway 40 is a major thoroughfare, we got to enjoy the soothing, natural sounds of tractor trailers down shifting as they topped the Divide all night. (Ah, wilderness!) Several edifice-sized semis were parked in the ski area lot within 100 feet of our tent almost until dawn — engines running the whole time — while their owners apparently caught a few winks. I sure hope they slept comfortably and well.

It was not the best kind of night to have before embarking on what ended up being the single hardest day of the Colorado section of the CDT. I mentioned there were two days that, before leaving on this hike, had me a little concerned because the words "trail undefined" appeared on my maps. The first of those days — when we climbed over Vasquez Peak — was a bear, and it was only a single "trail undefined" day. Today, we face two "trail undefineds," with a "trail undefined with exposure" tossed in for good measure. As if that wasn't bad enough on the pre-hike psychological front, this is the day we cross the CDT's highest point, 13,391-foot Parry Peak. In addition, we will cross three other 13,000-plus-foot peaks before the sun sets. Well, hopefully before the sun sets. It would have been nice to hit the trail rested and refreshed rather than feeling punch-drunk from lack of shut-eye. It took several hours before the roar of those truck engines dissipated from my mind's ear.

Once again, we have the opportunity to get limbered up right out of camp on a very steep dirt road, this one going up the side of Colorado Mines Peak. We are both stiff and slow, and it takes 45 minutes to make it one mile to the point where the trail takes leave of the dirt road, which continues on to the summit. From the trail, we can see the top, and it is covered with all sorts of military-looking antenna arrays. (For all I know, it's some sort of microwave relay station for the Playboy Channel.) Alongside the trail, which once again is not a trail but, rather, a series of cairns spread across the trackless tundra, someone has made a peace symbol from pieces of the bright-white quartz that has been decorating the tundra in abundance ever since Jones Pass. Perhaps, like me, the peace sign builder suspected that those antennas atop the peak have an ominous, non-peaceful, non-Playboy Channel purpose.

A lot of times, I fear I paint an inaccurate picture when I refer to "the Divide." I believe I make it sound like the Divide is a reasonably mellow ridge line that, once accessed, is fairly easy to hike along. In many places, such is certainly the case. But, in many other instances, the crest of the Divide itself is the least innocuous terrain for many miles. Often, the multi-thousand-foot, multi-hour, multi-heart attack ascent to the Divide is the part of your hiking day that you look back upon with the most fondness. This is one such section. Though not dangerous in the fall-to-your-death sense (yet), the Divide here consists of nothing save one very steep and deep, trailless ascent followed within three inches by one very steep and deep, trailless descent. And vice versa. And on and on. All of this, too, is above 12,000 feet.

As we crossed over Mount Flora and several close-by unnamed peaks and descended into the notches that separated them, our feet were either scrunched into the front thirds of our boots because of the severity of the downs or crammed into the back thirds of our boots because of the torturousness of the ups. The middle parts of our feet were feeling just fine, I am happy to report.

To the east, we could see far out onto the Great Plains. This is the easternmost meander of the Continental Divide in Colorado. One of the most striking things about the Rockies is that there is little in the way of graduality as you approach the mountains from the flatlands. You walk easily across the Plains until you run face-first into what is known as the Front Range. The City of Boulder — just east of us — is located at an elevation of about 5,500 feet. The town of Ward, 30 miles west of Boulder and still in Boulder County, is more than 9,000 feet high. From where we now stand, flatness is the dominant geographical feature as far as the eye can see. A featureless horizon is a strange sight after spending all these miles along the Divide. It's almost disorienting.

Directly below us, though, is a series of alpine lakes — Ethel, Byron, Bill Moore, Slater, Sherwin — that look as pristine as any I have seen on this hike. If I had more time, I would drop down and visit every single one of them. I hate to walk by an alpine lake without getting to know it a little. But we have to press on. I am already feeling behind schedule, but the going is necessarily deliberate.

The ground seemed to be on fire, as the tundra plants were in the bright-red height of their autumn glory. Most people do not equate fall colors with the tundra, because, not surprisingly, most people equate fall colors with trees, which are in mighty short supply at this altitude. But, for a few short weeks between dead of summer and the time when the tundra hunkers down in preparation for winter's merciless onslaught, the miniature plants that live up this high do their darnedest to

SUNRISE ON MOUNT FLORA, ARAPAHO NATIONAL FOREST

ETHEL LAKE

ICE LAKE, PROPOSED JAMES PEAK WILDERNESS

compete in a battle of brilliance with their larger plant brethren down below.

I could hardly take my eyes off the crimson carpet beneath my feet. I finally told Gay that, for all the world, this tundra seemed like a dryland equivalent of the bottoms of the small tidal pools that dot northern California's beaches. At this, Gay looked down at the ground, looked up at me, looked back down at the ground and wondered aloud if I had recently consumed some weird species of tundra mushroom. She told me that I ought to be spending more time looking up than down at this particular juncture.

She was right. A severe storm front was bearing down on us fast. The opaque cloud bank filled the western sky. End-to-end gray and nasty. We had already passed both of those "trail undefined" sections without mishap, but we still had to go over Mount Eva, Parry Peak, the flank of Mount Bancroft and James Peak. We also had that "trail undefined with exposure" section, which looked on the map to be a deep notch above Ice Lake between Bancroft and James.

As we plodded up Mount Eva, the storm hit us like something out of a J.R.R. Tolkien novel. We quickly found cover at the bottom of a small rock face and donned our rain gear. The temperature had dropped 30 degrees in 30 minutes. We snuggled together with Cali crammed between us as the rain beat down and the lightning crashed. "Enjoying your vacation?" I asked Gay. She only grunted, her face buried in the hood of her rain jacket.

Once the rain stopped, we quickly started hiking again, even though the storm obviously was going to be with us for a while yet. At the summit of Mount Eva was some sort of trashed-out, abandoned building. I ran over to check out the potential shelter-from-the-storm quotient, but the building was gutted and unusable, even by frightened backpacker standards, which aren't very high. Then it dawned on me that this building probably was once grounded as a precaution against lightning, but, now, it was torn apart with its metal components spread out scarecrow-style over several hundred square yards of treeless tundra. I decided this was no place for a lightning wuss to be hanging out, and we ran down the north side of the mountain, putting as much distance as possible between us and all that metal on the the summit of Mount Eva.

Halfway up Parry Peak, the storm hit again, and once more we had to rain gear-up and hunker down for 20 minutes. Unfortunately, I tore my pack raincover while slinging it around, and it was too wet to effect a meticulous, hyper-detailed field repair that only experienced, worldly and technically oriented backpackers are trained to perform (otherwise known as "applying a whole bunch of duct tape to the tears").

By the time we reached the summit of the highest point along the entire 3,100-mile Continental Divide National Scenic Trail, we were socked in so bad we could not see 50 feet. We could still make out the last cairn we passed on the way up, but we could not see the next cairn ahead. We had no idea whether the trail descended

ICEBERG BELOW THE DIVIDE

the northern and eastern slope of Parry Peak, and we didn't want to take any chances. We had no alternative except to wait the storm out on the exact tip-top of a 13,300-foot mountain.

We huddled next to a small rock wall someone had built on the summit. After a few minutes, the storm abated, but the clouds still remained. The air was still, and there was no rain or lightning. It was like we were in a dory fogged in off the Maine coast. There was nothing to do but sit and wait.

We just lay back and relaxed. Gay and I have been neck-deep in so many variations on the not-perfectly-comfortable theme while backpacking that dealing with things like high-altitude fog-ins barely fazes us. Sure, we would both rather have the sun shining with the temperature hovering somewhere around 70. But, there's always a yin-yang cosmic mountain formula at play in the Rockies. When a storm clears, the alpine wilderness is at its most gorgeous, and it only achieves that degree and kind of gorgeousness after a storm. There is no way you can interface with the sensory best that the High Country has to offer without dealing head-on with Mother Nature at her most intense. Thing is, Mother Nature at her most intense is worth the visit in and of itself. John Steinbeck once wrote words to this effect in *Travels with Charlie*: "I don't like climate; I like weather." I agree. I'm not as nutso as John Muir was — I mean, I don't climb tall trees during a thunderstorm or anything. Still, I have no problems whatsoever with hunkering down on top of a very tall mountain in the middle of nowhere while a funky bit of weather passes over — as long as there's no close-at-hand lightning. (That's when I want my mommy.) In a place like the Colorado High Country, you can do more than just watch and appreciate the beauty and power of passing storms from a distance; you can also sit inside a storm as it moves by. You can reach out and touch the inner workings of the machine that produces lightning, thunder, rain and snow.

As the storm began to break up, we saw that the air had not really been calm at all — it had only been calm around us. A few feet away, the clouds were whizzing by, and, as the patches of clear, blue sky finally started breaking through, neither of us could move. The scene was so mesmerizingly beautiful, we could not draw air into our lungs. We held hands and just waited for the show to end. When it did, we took off fast down toward the notch between Parry Peak and Mount Bancroft. We de-rain-geared, as the sun had broken out full force. Then

ICE LAKE

we promptly lost the trail as it traversed Bancroft. I took an educated guess that may have been educated, but it was still wrong. We spent 15 minutes stumbling through a boulder field before seeing a cairn. We were only minutes from the dreaded "trail undefined with exposure." Now, though, our primary concern was lack of water, as we had passed nary a drop all day. The plan was to go 11.7 miles from Berthoud Pass to a small spring on the other side of James Peak we had read about. As far as we knew, that was the first and only water we would pass this day. But it was already two o'clock, and we still had to deal with the undefined and exposed trail ahead as well as crossing 13,294-foot James Peak.

The trail meandered to the northeast flank of Mount Bancroft, and we finally laid eyes on the undefined exposure. Our eyes could not believe themselves. We faced the steepest, longest, fashionably trail-free descent of the day into a small notch that was surrounded by ridiculous ups on two sides and impossible downs on the other two sides. But, since we had been mentally preparing ourselves for this all day, the descent went fast and well. The other side was another story. A series of cairns had been dropped at random from an airplane into the middle of an entire mountainside's-worth of crumbly, loose, high, precipitous rocks. There was nothing to do except press on and play Spiderman. After several series of technical rock-climbing moves, I started to get seriously nervous. I was becoming fatigued almost as quickly as I was getting dehydrated. Gay had never done any hand-over-hand scrambling, much less with a bulky external-frame pack. And Cali looked up ahead and almost swallowed her tongue. Despite her inexperience, Gay was moving very strongly and confidently. I took Cali's pack off her and strapped it to my Gregory. Since the mutt's pack contained four days' worth of food, it weighed about 12 pounds — enough extra weight that it felt like a neutron star had landed on top of my shoulders. It was all I could do to keep from falling over backward.

The climb out of the notch, which, as far as I can tell, is inexplicably nameless (I thought of a few potential names, but none of them are printable), was not easy. I had to pick Cali's 55-pound carcass up several times and place her on a ledge over my head. I hit my cumbersome pack several times and almost lost my balance in places that would have pretty much driven home the definition of "exposure."

By the time we made it out of the notch, the thought of going much further was unappealing. But, we were completely dry. We had to keep hiking until we crossed water or, failing that, a sizeable patch of snow. We were at more than 13,000 feet, and the higher you are, the faster you dehydrate.

Then, a miracle happened just before we began climbing James Peak: We crossed a wonderful little snowmelt stream. As another thick bank of dark clouds moved in, we decided to make camp. We had only gone seven or so miles, but, right then, I would trade distance for water.

JAMES PEAK

129

John Fayhee on Parry Peak

Gay Gangel-Fayhee

Photographing Ice Lake

Dave Nessia

I have never camped in a place this high or wild feeling. I am exhilarated. Some tundra, though serious business and all because of the elevation, feels benign, even friendly. This whole section of trail from Berthoud Pass has felt intensely ominous. I can't say that I feel comfortable here. But I still feel glad to be here. Cali and I go for a post-dinner walk to a precipice that drops straight down for many thousand feet into the Fraser River Valley. To the left lies the north face of Parry Peak. I am very glad we did not press on in that direction during our fog-in experience; we would have died very shortly after leaving the summit.

I get up in the middle of the night and am shocked to see the entire Metro Denver skyline below me. The lights of civilization fill the plains in every direction. It is spellbinding and repugnant at the same time.

I learned several months later that the Forest Service has decided to take the Divide Trail off this ridge specifically to avoid that nameless notch. As a result, the trail will now miss Parry Peak. The CDT's highest point will no longer be its highest point, and the trail will now follow a series of dirt roads well below the east side of the Divide. It seems that the Forest Service believes this stretch of trail is too tough and dangerous for the general public. The gentrification of the CDT has started. Maybe I feel this way because I made it through the notch unscathed, and, more importantly, so did my wife.

If Gay and I can make it through that notch with full packs and a dog, then anyone who has any business hiking on the Divide Trail in the first place ought to be able to make it through. I have heard numerous people say words to the effect that the Divide Trail needs to be designed and constructed in such a way that the average person can enjoy it. Poppycock. If there is any one trail in this country that ought to be designed and constructed in such a way as to preclude premeditatedly the average person, the CDT is it. This is not the Colorado Trail — which was specifically designed to be easy — or some five-mile loop around a state park in Connecticut. This is the Divide Trail, and that is a footpath of a whole "nuther" color. We cannot allow this trail to be completed with the lowest common denominator outdoorsperson in mind or, for that matter, even the average common denominator.

This may sound like I want the CDT to be built and maintained as some sort of private personal playground for the fit and experienced. But I have worked hard for a lot of years to get to the point where I can handle something as arduous and intense as the CDT. I do not believe that should be taken away

Big place!

Dave Nessia

from me or anyone else who has dedicated their lives to mastering the skills necessary to not get killed in the roughest of backcountry locales. There ought to be at least one of our long-distance National Scenic Trails set up for people not only willing but eager to rub elbows with the baddest stuff the Rockies can dish up. And now we have a move to take the big-daddy of all American hiking trails down off the Divide onto a series of nasty dirt roads simply because Joe Blow the Schmo from Pocono might not be able to deal safely with one gnarly stretch of trail.

The Appalachian Trail Powers That Be are probably laughing in their beer at this one, as the AT has a mile-long stretch of extremely dangerous boulders in Maine called Mahoosic Notch — which is much harder to hike through than the notch above Ice Lake. All AT end-to-end hikers measure their trip in pre- and post-Mahoosic Notch terms. This should be the Mahoosic Notch of the CDT forever.

John Fayhee and Cali

Gay Gangel-Fayhee

This should be the section by which all CDT hikers measure their trek.

A Forest Service person told me that the difficulty of the section was not the only reason why the trail was being moved down from the Divide. She told me that it would be almost impossible to build durable tread through a section that steep and rugged. When I suggested that maybe the route simply

SOUTH FORK MIDDLE BOULDER CREEK, INDIAN PEAKS WILDERNESS

ought to be left as it is, she repeated the long-held belief that, once the Divide Trail is completed and marked and accurately mapped and corporately sponsored, more and more people will know about it and, therefore, use it. And increased use, she said, would surely take its toll on the heretofore fairly pristine tundra. Maybe all that's true. But maybe the way around this trail-location conundrum is to simply leave the CDT as it is, mark it, map it and advertise it not one whit more than it already is. At that suggestion, the Forest Service person looked at me like I must have recently received a sharp whop on the head by a sledgehammer. I understood that look; it is the same look you see everywhere in Colorado these days when the suggestion of simply leaving well enough alone is made. Leaving things in their current state of primitiveness simply does not jive with the aforementioned monument-building mentality that is now dominating the Colorado mindset.

I guess the simple act of moving the CDT down from the Divide to a series of dirt roads passing through the trees will not prohibit hardier hikers from taking the Parry Peak/unnamed-killer-notch route, but, when you're hiking a long trail, you generally feel somewhat obligated to stay on that trail, no matter where it goes.

Before dawn, Gay took a picture-taking walk back toward the notch. Down below she could see cars and trucks parked near Loch Lomond, right where the new and improved version of the CDT will be located.

As we approached Rollins Pass — the southern boundary of the magnificent Indian Peaks Wilderness, I pulled out Cali's leash for the first time in many miles. In Colorado, the 73,391-acre Indian Peaks is doggie-in-the-wilderness-issue ground zero.

A few weeks before leaving on this hike, Gary and I had taken a two-day shakedown cruise into the Sangre de Cristo Wilderness. On the way in, I could tell something was bothering Gary. It took a little prodding, but eventually it came out that he was irritated by the fact that I planned to bring Cali along with us on the CDT.

This surprised me, as Gary is an avowed dog lover who happens to own three curs back in Michigan. The difference was, he told me, that he had chosen to leave his dogs at home, while I was bringing mine with us as we tromped through the middle of Colorado's most remote and pristine wilderness and backcountry areas. He said he did not mind having the dog along for social reasons; rather, he had environmental concerns at heart. He said he believes the backcountry, especially legally designated wilderness areas, ought to be off-limits to dogs because of the alleged havoc they wreak on wildlife and the natural world.

Certainly, this was not the first time I had had such arguments laid on me, but it was the first time a self-professed dog lover had brought them up in such an overtly confrontational manner. I had a whole slew of well-reasoned (at least I hoped) responses to Gary's points, most of which centered around the fact that I had worked long and hard to teach Cali good trail manners. By and large, she stays close

PINK INDIAN PAINTBRUSH, INDIAN PEAKS WILDERNESS

DEVILS THUMB LAKE, INDIAN PEAKS WILDERNESS

Dwarf spruce, Indian Peaks Wilderness

CAMP ON JASPER CREEK, INDIAN PEAKS WILDERNESS

to me, obeys my commands instantly and leaves wildlife, most of which she is afraid of anyway, alone.

Gary's points, unfortunately, were framed in a context that transcended my hike with Cali along the CDT. They were, rather, framed in a context called "Colorado," where the acrimony between dog owners and non-dog owners has reached such contentious proportions that the Roosevelt-Arapaho National Forest is considering a total, 100-percent dog ban in several of the wilderness areas it administers. The Indian Peaks, being the Roosevelt-Arapaho's showcase wilderness area, as well as being one of the busiest wildernesses in the Rockies, is at the heart of the controversy.

The last thing I want to do is contribute to this situation, so, for the six miles we pass through the Indian Peaks, Cali is kept on a short leash. She seems mightily perturbed and confused.

We stop just below Devils Thumb Pass for a snack, but the wind is blowing so hard we opt to press on. During the three-mile descent into Devil's Thumb Park, where we plan to camp, we lose 2,100 vertical feet. Just like that, we are back in the trees, and the hardest part of the whole hike is behind us. It finally is starting to sink in that this adventure is quickly winding down. All of the Colorado CDT superlatives are now behind me — the highest peaks, the section with the highest average elevation, the longest stretch and the most arduous stretch. It's almost time to go home, and that thought makes

JOHN FIELDER CHANGES FILM HOLDERS

DAVE NESSIA

me feel sick to my stomach. I am now completely comfortable living on the trail. I feel like I could happily stay out here for many more weeks.

We were also now back in the hiking mainstream. There were dozens of groups camped near Devils Thumb Park — a marshy, multi-hundred-acre meadow — so we walked back in the woods a short distance and found a decent spot atop a small rise next to a nameless brook. We were worried about Cali, as she seemed to be developing a lame shoulder. I have been going back and forth about whether or not to send her home for the summer once we reach Grand Lake. She has more than 400 miles under her belt and has done a wonderful job, as well as proving to be a great hiking partner. But she is still less than a year old, and I fear that, if she stays on the trail with me after Gay returns home, she might begin to wonder if we're ever going home, or if this is to be her life forevermore. If she stays lame, the decision will be made for me.

The mostly level trail now winds its way through deep woods and along well-marked abandoned logging roads. It is pleasant hiking to Monarch Lake, which is on the edge of the Arapaho National Recreation Area. It is Labor Day weekend, so we are prepared to interact with the teeming masses. After considerable effort, we find one barely usable campsite right above Monarch Lake, and we try to lay low, because, undoubtedly, we are breaking some sort of National Park Service anti-camping-near-the-lake regulation. I generally avoid national parks like the plague, because I think the Park Service is what every land stewardship agency would be like if the Nazis had won the war. But tonight we have no choice but to stay on Park Service turf. It will not surprise us if we are arrested at gunpoint for some administrative infraction.

Since the trail passes through Rocky Mountain National Park —

ON THE TRAIL, INDIAN PEAKS WILDERNESS

where dogs are strictly prohibited — I leave Gay and Cali at a recreation area campground and literally run the 12 miles to Grand Lake where our truck is parked. It takes only three hours to get to Grand Lake and another hour to get back to my wife and dog. They have spent the afternoon dozing in the sun and listening to the omnipresent sound of motorboats zooming around in a holiday-weekend frenzy on nearby Lake Granby.

By late afternoon, we are safely ensconced in the cabin of our friend Aurel Burtis, whose family has owned property in Grand Lake for 50 years. The plan is to spend two full days in town eating, resting and eating some more. This is the end of the CDT line for Gay, and, since I have decided after all to send Cali home with her, I will be hiking the four days from Grand Lake to Muddy Pass by myself.

I lived for almost two years in this picturesque hamlet, which is located on the north shore of its namesake lake, the state's largest natural body of water. This is the place where I first rubbed elbows with the High Country. Truth be told, it intimidated the hell out of me. I lived here during the infamous winter of 1983–84, which, for

DAVE SANDERS ON THE DIVIDE

JOHN FAYHEE TAKES A BREAK

GAY GANGEL-FAYHEE

ALPINE WILDFLOWERS, ROCKY MOUNTAIN NATIONAL PARK

my generation, set the standard by which all winters since have been judged. By the first week of November, we had received nary a flake of snow. When the white stuff finally came on November 8, it came with a vengeance that left the entire region stupefied. By December 28, we had had 300 inches. On Christmas day alone we had four feet. It took me six hours to dig my car out. But, by the first of the year, the snow had pretty much stopped for the season. Then the cold came. We had two separate five-day stretches when the temperature dipped to minus-50 at night. And we're not talking about any wimpy child-chill-factor stuff; we're talking about pure, unadulterated frigidity in the extreme. It took six years for me to get up the nerve to winter again in the High Country.

This is also where I met Gay, and it was here that I proposed to her. During my two-day break from the CDT, we took a hand-in-hand stroll down memory lane, walking by the very place where I popped THE question (as every married person knows, there is, after all, only one real question in life), and it felt good to realize that, in the 13 years since we first met and fell in love, we have moved up from being hovel renters to slum owners.

Gay drove me out to North Supply trailhead. When she pulled away with Cali, I was alone for the first time on this hike, and that felt both good and liberating. Now I can sing as loudly as I want and toss social decorum to the four winds without offending anyone. Actually, it is with a profound sense of relief that I was without company. At least half of all the thousands of days I have spent backpacking have been by my lonesome. It may not necessarily be my overall favorite way to backpack, but many times it is. This is one of those times.

Gay knew I was looking forward to having these four days by myself. She, like me, has a streak of hermit in her, so she understands the concept of the aggressive pursuit of solitude. I believe Gay had a marvelous time hiking with me from Summit County to Grand Lake, but I also believe she was ready to part ways with me for a while. Several times she had to remind me as I snapped at her for one unjustified petty reason or another that she was not Gary. I obviously needed some time alone for some negativity purging.

There was a well-used campsite right at the North Supply trailhead, so I quickly set up my tent and spent the evening savoring the three cans of Spaghetti-Os I had bought at a gas station/convenience store earlier in the day. You know you are in a food-oriented frame of mind when you are treating greasy, flavor-free canned pasta as though it were a four-star meal served atop a linen tablecloth by a drop-dead

Cony Creek, Rocky Mountain National Park

gorgeous waitress. By this point, I was constantly ravenous, which was not surprising, as I learned in Grand Lake that I had lost almost 30 pounds since Cumbres Pass. My body fat ratio was hovering somewhere in the negative percentage range. I was thinking of food constantly and had even had several dreams about diving head-long into and doing the breaststroke through entire swimming pools filled with spareribs, cookies and Snickers bars.

This 54-mile stretch is the only part of the hike that is not planned on a day-by-day basis. I have good maps, but this is the other area besides Summit County that has CDT location problems. But, unlike Summit, there aren't even temporary or alternate routes through much of this section. This is a leap of faith, and I just assume I will find comfortable accommodations at the end of each trail day. Since I am by my lonesome, this situation does not even faze my normally anal-retentive, detailed-planning-based self.

Shortly after breaking camp at the crack of 8:30 (when I am by myself, I never get an early start), I pass two CDT through-hikers. This marks the first time all summer I am not the alpha-dog in the trail pecking order. These two gentlemen left Montana two months before and planned to cross the Mexican border sometime in November. They were seriously lean and mean, and looked like they had visited neither a tailor nor a beautician in at least several days. They told me they were getting up every morning at 4:30, were hiking by 5:00 and were averaging almost 30 miles a day. I was humbled. When I told them I was hiking only from New Mexico to Wyoming and that I had been out for 52 days and almost 600 miles, they looked at me almost condescendingly. But, if anyone has a right to do that, it's CDT through-hikers. Tail between my legs, I wished them happy trails and slinked off toward Wyoming, where my inconsequential hike would end.

One of the best things about Colorado is that it boasts innumerable lesser known nooks and crannies that are absolutely spectacular. The Never Summer Wilderness is one such place. With Rocky Mountain National Park so close, most people don't even consider visiting this small wilderness area. Yet, only a few miles from the trailhead, the CDT passes into a landscape of rugged, wonderful and seldom-visited tundra. The trail goes through the Never Summer for only a couple of miles, but all along Blue Ridge — past Bowen Lake, Cascade and Ruby mountains, Bowen Pass and finally into the headwaters of Illinois Creek — the views are stunning and clear all the way back to James and Parry peaks.

On my way down from Blue Ridge, I ran into two more CDT through-hikers. This was a couple from Florida, and they were a little less condescending in their demeanor than the boys I passed earlier. We actually sat down and traded information about the trail. This couple had also noticed the words "trail undefined with exposure" on their map and were wondering what sort of adventures awaited them. When I related the topographical situation, they nodded and pointed west, toward Parkview Mountain and told me to prepare myself. "Parkview Mountain?" I asked, incredulously. Sounded like something garden clubs climb in Massachusetts or England. I had never even heard of Parkview Mountain, yet there it was on the western horizon, looking as benign as a pile of cotton candy. This couple also pointed northward. "There's Wyoming, right there," the male said. My heart stopped. As the couple walked away toward Mexico, I just sat there for a few minutes both savoring and fearing the thought of my journey's end. It couldn't be coming to a close this quickly; there were still too many thoughts to think and misadventures to experience.

From that point on, my hike along the Colorado section of the CDT was a different thing than it had been before. From the moment I saw Wyoming, I knew beyond the shadow of a reasonable doubt that I was going to make it unscathed to the Cowboy State. From here, I could hobble, limp or crawl to the end of this most wonderful of walks through the Colorado woods.

I had planned to camp somewhere along Illinois Creek, but decided to press on over Illinois Pass. It was pleasant to be able to make that decision without having to consider the desires or feelings of anyone else. I made it several miles down Trout Creek and camped in a sun-dappled and secluded aspen grove. The air smelled like autumn, and I consider that smell the most invigorating in the world. It's even better than the smell of bacon and eggs cooking in the wilderness. For years, I sort of worried about my intense love of fall because it is, after all, the season of withering and death. But I have come to understand that I don't love fall in any conceptual or metaphorical sense. Rather, I love it purely for its sensations — the smells, the feel of the dry, crisp air and the changing colors. It's not like I am glad summer has passed or that I am glad winter is approaching. I love fall for itself. Plus, during September, there are few people out and about in the backcountry, and the bugs have bugged off. Optimum time in an optimum place.

I crossed Highway 125 at Willow Creek Pass and, during a snack break, noticed that I was due to start climbing this twinky-sounding Parkview Mountain almost

Longs Peak (14,255') and Mount Meeker

SUNRISE ON HALLETT PEAK

immediately. Admittedly, the numbers on the map seemed reasonably impressive: 2,700 feet in 2.5 miles. Hmmm. . . That's more than 1,000 feet per mile, and generally ascents start getting fairly captivating at about a 500-feet-per-mile grade. Still, I'm in terrific shape, and I've breezed up lots of more intense mountains than this on the CDT.

Two hours later, the only thing dragging farther back than my tongue was my ego. For several miles, the trail followed a ridiculously steep and dusty dirt road. By this time, I had decided to stop for the night at the first water, and I fervently hoped to pass a nice flower-lined brook on the Willow Creek Pass side of Parkview. But the entire eastern side of the mountain was parched. I had to cross the summit. From the point where the dirt road ended and the cairns (what else?) began, Parkview showed its true nature. For a half mile, it became near vertical. I tried hard to avoid walking uphill on my tippy-toes, because of the negative impact on the Achilles' tendons and calves. But here I could not avoid it. For an hour, my heels never touched terra firma. I was taking 10 steps, then lying down and sleeping for 12 hours, then taking another 10 steps.

Somewhere over toward Summit County, there are a couple of CDT through-hikers from Florida who are laughing their heads off at the thought of the cavalier attitude I displayed when they told me about this mountain.

When I finally made it to the long-disused fire lookout on the summit, I collapsed in a heap. My hamstrings almost seized up, and I felt a case of terminal cramps getting ready to erupt in my calves. But the wind was so strong, I decided to hike on. The drop down Parkview's west side was no less forgiving. My thighs felt like they were going to explode and my toes were getting banged so badly they were being shoved back under the front of my feet.

By the time I got to a small saddle 1,000 feet below the summit, I had had it for the day. I dropped my pack in a grove of pines right at treeline and headed down into a small side drainage looking for water. Ten minutes later I came across enough of a trickle that I could fill my water bag. Just as I was about to step down next to a plate-size pool, a huge boulder I was standing on came loose and, the next thing I knew, I was looking at my feet silhouetted against the azure sky. A nanosecond later, I landed hard enough on my rump that my teeth cracked together so severely I saw several small planets orbiting around my spinning head. It took a few moments to inventory my body parts mentally, making certain that nothing was broken. It is moments like these that make a person appreciate the concept of solitude; it would have been awful to have a witness to this mishap.

But that's the thing about hiking alone in the middle of seldom-used nowhere. If I suffered a broken leg, it would be several days before anyone would even think to start looking for me, and, even then, they would have to search 30 miles of trail, which I would not be on, because I'm down here in this little side drainage. I guess

COLORADO COLUMBINE ABOVE ARROWHEAD LAKE, ROCKY MOUNTAIN NATIONAL PARK

NEVER SUMMER MOUNTAINS

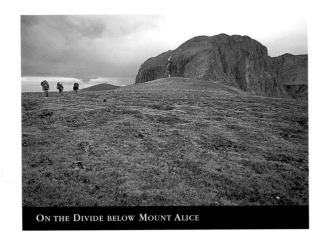

ON THE DIVIDE BELOW MOUNT ALICE

eventually someone would notice my purple Gregory leaning against that pine up on the ridge. Sooner or later, someone would find me — dead or alive.

When I get back to my pack, I notice it's getting hazy. Fearing an approaching storm, I quickly pitch my tent and get camp ready for rain. Then I notice the smell of smoke. To the west, past Haystack Mountain and through the high cloud cover, I can barely make out a towering plume. There's obviously a large fire blazing away pretty much where I expect to be hiking the next day. I mean, my map might as well have dispensed with the traditional "west" delineation and told me simply to take a compass bearing off all that smoke over there near Haystack Mountain. That would be my luck, to expire in a fire seven hiking days from Wyoming.

I spend the afternoon alternately reading Pat Conroy's *The Prince of Tides* and fretfully eyeballing the smoke-filled western horizon. I am friends with a fair number of professional forest-fire fighters, and therefore have heard some frightening stories over the years concerning the vagaries of wilderness conflagrations. I wonder if I should pack up and head back over the summit of Parkview while the getting is good. Thing is, I believe I would rather perish in a sea of flames than climb and descend that blasted mountain again.

All afternoon and evening, one awesome cloud bank after another crossed the Divide. It stormed viciously all around, but not a single drop of rain landed on me. Twice, huge sunny holes opened up in the clouds and passed directly over me. Both times, it seemed like I was about to experience either some sort of fairly major spiritual event or be abducted by an alien spacecraft. Nothing of that sort transpired, so I just sat there thanking my lucky weather stars. For once. Most times, if there is a single small cloud within sight, it will hunt me down and find a way to squeeze at least one drop of rain out, and it will target that raindrop over me like a torpedo bomber targets a ship at sea. But, this go-round, the rain spirits were being cool, and I was consequently dry, warm and very comfortable. Just as I thought that thought, I spaced out and used my cup of tea for an ashtray, ruining both my pre-supper hot beverage and my cigar. So, all was pretty much well and normal with the cosmos after all.

The next morning, the smoke was still there. It didn't seem to have gotten any worse, so I nervously continued along the Divide.

Parkview Mountain was not named after Fred Parkview. To the north, the view of North Park opened up in its enormous entirety. Pancake-flat, North Park fills a wide plain between the northern Mummy Range and the Zirkels. The extractive industries hereabouts are as politically and culturally dominant as the ski industry in my home county. For the past few days, there have been signs of massive timbering both recent and old. It is repulsive, and I can't wait to get out of this area.

By the end of the day, I have crossed ominously named Poison Ridge (where, inexplicably, many of the trees are dead as doornails) and dropped off the Divide into the Middle Fork drainage. Mark Fox is set to bring me a food drop the next

ON THE TRAIL

day at the Hyannis Peak trailhead, and I want to get as close to the place where my chow will be delivered as possible before nightfall. At 6:30, I pitch my tent in a barely flat area right on the side of the trail. A heavy thunderstorm moves in, and it pours all night. During the night, I can smell smoke. Either there is someone else camping nearby, or the fire I saw from Parkview Mountain is still smoldering somewhere close by.

By morning everything is soaked through. Since I figure I am only two miles from the trailhead, I sleep in and cook breakfast while miserably sitting in my tiny tent.

Ten minutes after breaking camp, a heavy animal tension suddenly fills the lush and wet woods. Something powerful has just arrived. The last time I had this feeling, I saw a mountain lion. I look quickly to my left and see a young bull moose sauntering through a meadow. He sees me and runs like the wind. For all their heft, moose can flat-out haul hooves. He is gone almost as soon as the information that I have just seen a moose registers in my brain. I don't see him again, but I follow fresh moose tracks most of the way to the trailhead. This is the first moose I have seen in Colorado, and, though the weather remains wet, cold and generally miserable until Mark arrives at 1 p.m., because of that one short animal interaction, my day is made; my trip is made.

But I now only have six days left on that trip.

ON HAGUES PEAK (13,560')

JON OSBORNE ON THE EDGE

NEVER SUMMER MOUNTAINS

Lake Granby from the Rabbit Ears Range

VII

MUDDY PASS TO THE WYOMING BORDER

The Mount Zirkel Wilderness

I had a queasy feeling that no good was going to come from my visit to the Forest Service office in Steamboat Springs, where I was taking my last day off the trail. Yet, since my motel was right across the street from the ranger station, I thought it would be both prudent and responsible of me to venture in to talk some CDT directional skinny with the staff.

My fretfulness proved justified, as the ranger on duty gave me the worst of all possible information: The CDT, he said, was so well-marked "you couldn't lose it if you tried." As soon as those words were uttered, I made the sign of the cross with my fingers in front of the ranger's perplexed face. But it was too late. The fateful words had been spoken, and I knew I was doomed beyond possible redemption. It would have been much better if he had told me the trail was unmarked, undefined, ugly as sin and populated by legions of well-armed, hiker-hating mass murderers. As I left the ranger office, I might as well have immediately paid someone to hog-tie me, put a sack over my head and drive me 12 hours in an unknown direction and leave me on the side of an unmarked dirt road in the middle of nowhere in the middle of the night. With those seven seemingly harmless words, that ranger was fating me to get lost. It was just a matter of where, when and how badly.

This karmic whammy could not have come at a worse public relations time. My friend Chris Nelson was planning to join me on this 62-mile stretch, and, if I got us in a locational pickle, he, being a guy and all, would be only too happy to relate the tale in great detail to everyone I knew back in Summit County. And who could blame him?

It rained hard the whole time I was in Steamboat, and I was not enthusiastic about returning to a wet trail. But, as Mark Fox and I drove on Highway 40 toward Muddy Pass and Dumont Lake Campground, where I was to meet Chris later in the day, we suddenly broke through the clouds into sunshine and warmth. After Mark left, I lazily whiled the day away reading, smoking and savoring every slice of the two extra-large pizzas I brought back from Steamboat Springs.

Chris arrived with a couple of bundles of wood, which was nice, as I had not built a fire all summer. I wistfully remember the days when campfires were de rigueur on backpacking trips. But in this day when environmental micro-sensitivity justifiably permeates every camping moment, I have bought into the notion of foregoing both the literal and figurative warmth of a crackling campfire. Too many areas are being denuded by firewood gathering, and that is very bad for topsoil regeneration. At the same time, unsightly campfire rings are causing damage in far too many backcountry locales.

In the decade or so since I eschewed campfire building, I have come to appreciate a lot of things that were lost on me during all those years when I would spend entire evenings staring at the hypnotic flames as though they were the backcountry equivalent of a TV set. (Predictable plot, but interesting dialogue.) Now, I see the stars and hear the nighttime music of the forest a lot better. I hit the sack earlier, and I don't smell like smoke constantly unless, of course, you count cigar smoke, which I don't, but my wife does.

Still, when Chris unloaded the wood, I smiled and looked forward to an old-fashioned evening sitting around the fire shooting the breeze and enjoying three or four cheap stogies. Sadly, we didn't have so much as a twig of kindling between us, so the only thing we got out of our fire-building efforts was complete smoke-smell saturation that did not go away for a week. The thing is, Chris arrived smelling like smoke, so he wasn't bothered in the least. Being a professional fireman, he had been called to fight the very blaze I had seen smouldering from the west side of Parkview Mountain. It ended up being only one drainage away from where I camped the night before I saw the moose. If it had not deluged that night, I might have awakened to flames lapping at my feet.

Chris and I had talked for many years about taking a long hike together. Though he is more a hunter/fisherman than a classic backpacker-type, he still appreciates the notion of taking long walks in the woods for no other reason than to walk in the woods. Unlike many "sportsmen," he doesn't feel compelled to try to kill something every time he walks away from a trailhead.

The next morning, we had three miles of dirt road before arriving at Base Camp trailhead. Halfway down the road, my friend Tom Jones, author of *Colorado's Continental Divide Trail: The Official Guide*, drove by out of the blue. He asked if we wanted a ride to the trailhead, and we were loaded up in his truck and ready to roll before he even finished posing the question.

Tom was dropping his vehicle off at Base Camp, and a friend of his, who was just behind us in his Subaru, planned to take him around to the Wyoming line, where he had some guidebook fine-tuning scheduled. He would be hiking back to Base Camp in a week or so. Within moments of

TARN, MOUNT ZIRKEL WILDERNESS

our arrival at the trailhead, Chris and I hoisted our packs and started walking as Tom and his friend drove away. The obvious trail took off from the dirt road and descended in a delightfully mellow fashion into a lush valley along a gurgling little stream. The trail was a tad more ratty than I had expected. It was fairly badly eroded and we had to cross over or around frequent blowdowns. But we still made good time, and the morning was so beautiful and the terrain so gentle we didn't mind a few obstacles. By this juncture, I was in the best shape I had been in since finishing the Appalachian Trail 16 years prior, back when I was young. I easily could have knocked off this stretch in three days, but really wanted to take my time and savor the last week of my hike. Since Chris hadn't had the chance to do much hiking in the previous few months, we were both perfectly content to saunter along at a 10-mile-per-day clip.

The trail was becoming less well-defined by the minute, and, by the time we stopped for a midmorning snack, I was starting to think — for the billionth time since leaving Cumbres Pass — that something was directionally amiss. But, practicing some serious male locational denial, we kept hiking until the trail disappeared completely in a vast, marshy meadow. I scanned the far side and could see neither cairns, blazes nor trail signs. My Steamboat Springs ranger station whammy had head-butted me right out of the chute. If there was no way I could lose the trail, then where was the trail I had obviously just lost? Embarrassed, I asked Chris to drop his pack while I began a circumnavigation of the meadow, hoping to stumble on some sign that another human had ever passed this way. But I was not optimistic. After an hour, I was flustered, frustrated and humiliated. I told Chris that I was almost ready to resign myself to hiking back out to the trailhead. But I sat down with my map and tried to relax, compose myself and figure out a tactful way to extricate us from this mess. To his credit, Chris had not laughed at me or called me names a single time. Yet.

Since Trails Illustrated marks treed areas in green and non-treed areas in white, I was able to find a clearing on the map that had the same shape as the meadow we were sitting in. I matched a couple of other map features to the surrounding terrain and let Chris know I felt fairly confident I knew where we were and where we had to go. I told him that, if we did not intersect the trail within a half-hour, we would have to hike out and start over. The bushwhacking was easy and, 20 minutes later, we came across the CDT. I didn't know if I should be pleased at my problem-solving acumen or irritated at my ability to get us lost in the first place where it supposedly was impossible to get lost.

The trail, which was so meticulously groomed it looked like it had been constructed by people who planned to eat Thanksgiving dinner off it, passed through some aspen-dominated woods that were just about to enter their fall-magnificence stage. A lot of easterners look down their noses at autumn in the Rockies, but I would trade without compunction a lifetime of Vermont maples for a 10-minute stroll through a golden-leafed grove of aspens in the heart of

Moss campion, Mount Zirkel Wilderness

DAWN TWILIGHT ALONG THE TRAIL

TREELINE CAMP, MOUNT ZIRKEL WILDERNESS

Colorado any day of the week. Something to do with the setting, for sure, but equally to do with the fact that aspens are magically beautiful in the fall. They don't just shine, they sparkle.

With only minimal topographical variation, this was some of the most pleasant walking I had experienced in weeks. The CDT from Base Camp trailhead to Buffalo Pass is one of the most popular rides for mountain bikers in this part of the state, and, since it was Sunday, we passed several dozen merry fat-tire enthusiasts. I was heartened by the overall friendliness and courtesy of the bikers we passed. Most stopped and chatted — a completely different scene from the one I confronted between Marshall and Monarch passes, seemingly 100 years and 1,000 miles ago.

We set up camp in a sweet-smelling meadow near Grizzly Lake. Our main evening activity consisted of speculating how this small lake might have come upon its name. Did someone see a grizzly here back in 1862? Did someone maybe get munched on by a grizzly here? If so, who and when? After all that conversational excitement, we both hit the sack by dusk. Chris was so tuckered out he was considering whether the process of crawling into his tent would actually be worth the effort, or whether he should just go ahead and sleep where he sat.

I learn this night that Chris, like Gary, is a snorer of some talent and consequence.

It took me a while to doze off as I was still irritated at having lost the trail earlier in the day. You would think by now that I could at least manage to stay on the trail during those rare occasions when there was trail to stay on. I'm sure Chris thinks I'm a boob of the first magnitude; I'm sure he's wondering how I managed to make it all the way from New Mexico in one piece. So much for impressing my pal with my backcountry prowess. I pondered potential retorts to the inevitable ribbing I was sure to suffer at the hands of my chums back home when word of this fiasco got back to them in Summit County. I hoped Chris had the common decency to do something embarrassing in the next five days, so we could blackmail each other into silence.

The fact that we had obviously gotten on the wrong trail immediately after Tom dropped us off ate at me for the rest of the hike. A month after I finished, I went back to Base Camp trailhead with Gay and learned that the CDT and its small trailhead sign had been blocked from view by Tom's friend's Subaru. We simply did not see it. Of course, neither did we look.

Before lunch the next day, we crossed into the 160,568-acre Mount Zirkel Wilderness at Buffalo Pass. This is one of the easiest treeline access points in the entire state. Within a mile of Buffalo Pass, we were strolling in some of the most pleasant tundra in Colorado. Buffalo Pass gets more precipitation than any other place in Colorado (with most of it coming in the winter), and this tundra looks more suited to family picnics than intense high-altitude backpacking. The grass is lush, the meadows are rolling and the rocks all look comfortable. And the demeanor of the trail fits right in with the laid-back landscape. It's a walk in the park. The

ARNICA

155

CDT through the Zirkels never goes above 12,000 feet, and, for the most part, it stays under 11,000. The biggest single vertical gain we will see for the next five days is a mere couple hundred feet. This is my CDT cool-down. I tell Chris how lucky he is to have chosen a place that is both easy and extremely scenic. Usually, it's one or the other, or, sometimes, neither.

The trail takes a miniscule turn for the worse near Lake Elbert, where, suddenly, we are following cairns across the tundra for what ends up being the last time. After crossing a small ridge finger, we find a rivulet above Luna Lake and kick back in the single most beautiful campsite I visited along the Colorado section of the CDT. We are about a half mile above treeline, and we can see Luna Lake in all its cobalt beauty down below. To the north is a boulder-strewn ridge and the Divide frames the sky to the east. It's so sunny we both wish for shade.

This is my last night up high on this hike, and I want to savor every morsel of the experience. The sunset lasts forever, and I stay up until the last tendrils of light have passed from the sky. It gets down to 20 degrees, and there's a whiff of winter in the morning air. I know 'tis the season to be thinking about moving down off the Divide. By mid-September in the High Country, severe snowstorms can come rolling in at any time without warning. Chris and I agree we would like to avoid having to work on our igloo-building skills.

On the way up Lost Ranger Peak the next morning, we pass several dozen of the most splendidly designed and constructed cairns I have ever seen. These are even better than the headstone-like cairns near Monarch Pass. Those were impressive, but they were all pretty much cut from the same mold, like the cairn-builder found a form he or she liked and ran with it. These cairns in the Zirkels are all individual works of art that are by and large more attractive than a lot of work I've seen displayed in galleries and museums. Each one is unique. Some are balancing act experiments, while others are built with miniature arches and windows. Still others look like animal-form-based sculptures. I wonder if one person did all of these, or whether it was one crew working in harmony together or several individuals competing against one another in an endless procession of cairn-building one-upmanship.

The hiking was so easy, we could not believe it when we arrived on the summit of Lost Ranger Peak, the high point of the Muddy-Pass-to-Wyoming stretch. How would you like to have a prominent peak in a well-used wilderness area named after one of your blunders? Everyone who comes up here must wonder about the story of the ranger who was so lost he had a mountain named after him. This poor schmuck probably was the best ranger in the entire state for 30 years, never once messing up and saving countless lives except for this one time, when there was a local mountain in need of a name. Can you imagine the shame? At least they didn't name it something more direct, like Lost Sam Jones Mountain or Stupid Sam Peak. So the ranger did not have to suffer the ultimate appellation indignity. But I can just imagine that there had to be a time or two in that anonymous ranger's life when he was sitting in a bar in Steamboat Springs or Walden and some stranger asked of the crowd, "Hey, anyone in here know how Lost Ranger Peak got its name?" And all eyes turn to Sam Jones, and the story gets told yet again.

From the summit, we cannot help but notice Mount Zirkel the highest point in its namesake wilderness area at 12,180 feet, flanked by Little Agnes Mountain and Big Agnes Mountain. I frantically fumble with my maps to make certain we do not have to pass through those babies. The northern part of the Zirkel Wilderness is the evil topographical twin of what we have been hiking through since leaving Buffalo Pass. Those three peaks run east-west rather than north-south, and they look so rugged as to actually appear frightening. Thankfully, we take a left before coming nose to nose with that formidable ridge.

When we started down into the Three Island Creek drainage, I stopped for one last look at the tundra. I don't know why I felt so sad about passing into the trees. I mean, I can see tons of tundra from my yard in Breckenridge and, within a 10-minute drive from my front door, I can be hiking or skiing above treeline. But this is the last tundra I will tromp through on this hike. The next time I walk above the trees, it will be a different thing entirely; it will be during the next stage of my life.

From the angle we approached Three Island Lake, where we planned to camp, we could see only one island, so, being mathematical geniuses, we assumed it wasn't Three Island Lake. But, just in case, we dropped our packs at a well-trampled campsite, and I walked around the lake to ask a couple of fisherpeople I could see if they knew which body of water this was. "Is this Three Island Lake?" I yelled out, not realizing until too late that, from the angle where the fisherpeople were, all three islands were easily visible. They looked at me like I was less than brilliant.

This is where the sportsman part of Chris' personality geysered its way out like Old Faithful. He sat in camp and watched fish hitting the surface of the lake for many minutes, the whole time licking his chops and mumbling over and over that he could not believe he came on this hike without a fishing pole. Several times, I thought he was going to jump in and try to catch a trout with his bare hands. I believe Chris was getting a tad tired of trail fare. I believe if he had the opportunity to prepare a little trout avec instant pork-flavored ramen, he would have done so in a skinny minute. And I might have invited myself over to his end of the campsite for dinner.

Two miles from Three Island Lake, we plow by a signless trail junction and end up walking an extra three miles on a hard gravel road.

PARRY PRIMROSE BELOW MOUNT ZIRKEL

THE SAWTOOTHS, MOUNT ZIRKEL WILDERNESS

This puts both of us in a bad mood and wreaks havoc on Chris' feet. He limps the rest of the way to Wyoming.

We are now in heavily pined, rolling hills, and the hiking is so tame my mind begins to wander. Unfortunately, it begins to wander in the direction of a conversation Chris and I had a few days prior. I had told him how, while Gay and I were walking through Bobtail Valley, out of the blue, a tune attached itself to my mind and would not let go. This would have been irritating enough if the tune in question was Bach's "Chaconne" or Haydn's "Emperor's Hymn" or something from the Beatles' White Album or even a song from the movie *Pulp Fiction*. But, no, the tune that repeated itself over and over inside my head was none other than "The Hokey Pokey." Mile after mile, for hours and hours and hours, I tried to purge that awful ditty from between my ears, but, the harder I tried, the louder it became. It would be one thing if I were intimately familiar with the subtle nuances of the entire Hokey Pokey libretto, but the only words I knew were, "You do the Hokey Pokey and you turn yourself around." (Is the turning around part of The Hokey Pokey, or is it some sort of required respite from The Hokey Pokey? And just what is The Hokey Pokey?)

Anyhow, I made the mistake of relating all this to Chris, who, with a mischievous smirk on his face, immediately began whistling the theme to the Andy Griffith Show, which may be the world's all-time worst melody when it comes to taking up residence in a person's mental sound system. The Hokey Pokey was gone, and for the rest of the hike I could have legitimately been addressed as Opie. I would have preferred to have some rousing musical score serve as the mental soundtrack finale

for this hike. Maybe something like Handel's "Messiah." But, no, I'm stuck with a cranial feedback loop of the Mayberry National Anthem. Figures.

The next day, we intersected an all-terrain-vehicle road, and, according to the maps, we would follow it all the way across the crest of the Sierra Madre to the Wyoming border. Trails designed for dirt bikes are usually fine, but ATV trails are always in terrible shape. This one sported one massive unavoidable quagmire after another. It was thoroughly unpleasant and, therefore, I made the decision to part ways with the Divide Trail a few miles short of Wyoming. I bent down, ran my fingers along the tread and pushed back a tear. Then I said adios to this wonderful footpath.

We followed the Trail Creek Trail across a small ridge and steeply descended into the valley of the West Fork of the Encampment River. We parked it for the night at massive West Fork Meadows. The rain moved in early, and it poured off and on all night and all morning.

Our gear was soaked. Since we only had three miles left to hike and since Gay was due to meet us late that afternoon at Lakeview Campground, I could have just tossed all my wet equipment haphazardly into my pack. But I went about all of my morning routines meticulously. A frantic feeling was welling up inside me. Tomorrow, I would be sleeping in my own bed. I would be off the trail. But I was not ready to leave the woods. I wanted to load up on supplies and keep on walking, just like I'd been doing for the past nine weeks.

All good hikes must come to an end, though, and my time was up.

The walk out was so easy I barely noticed it. I was hiking in a haze and a daze. Inside my head, the whole hike was playing itself back, minute by minute, step by step. I was so distracted, I could have walked right by a herd of giraffes and not seen them.

One side of me was happy; one side of me was sad. I was very pleased with the way I had physically, emotionally and spiritually held up for the past 740 miles.

I was overjoyed to have seen the territory I had seen. Yet, I was bummed that things had not worked out with Gary. I figured I would feel sad about that for a long while. Still, I felt as calm and balanced as I had in years. My internal batteries felt recharged in a way that can only come about after spending a long period of time not only out in Nature, but in mountainous Nature.

By 10:00, we were at Hog Park Trailhead, and, 200 yards later, we entered Wyoming at some signless point. I began the hike without a sign and ended it the same way. Seemed perfectly appropriate.

It took us two hours to hitch a ride to Lakeview Campground, and, by suppertime, Gay had arrived, right on schedule. She predictably brought with her several hundred thousand calories worth of wonderfully filling chow, which we really needed because we were totally food-free. We didn't even have a spoonful of instant coffee between us.

After another wet night, we packed up Gay's car and were on the road before dawn. On the way toward Steamboat Springs, we crossed the CDT. But this was Wyoming — that wasn't my CDT, at least not this time. Still, I almost jumped out of the car so I could keep on hiking. While on the Appalachian and Colorado trails, I could not wait to return to civilization. Whatever good I got from those trails, I got well before they ended. But I was not yet ready to leave this trail. Perhaps it's because this trail had not ended, only my time upon it. It continued north through

Wyoming, into Montana and Idaho, and, finally, to the Canadian border at a place I visited long ago in Glacier National Park, during the summer when those three people were killed by grizzlies.

Like it or not, it was time to leave behind the Colorado section of the Continental Divide National Scenic Trail and my journey upon that trail. It was time to rub elbows once more with civilization.

You can never go home again, but sometimes you have to.

M. John Fayhee

Two days after leaving the Continental Divide Trail, I was back in my office. I had no idea answering machines could hold that many messages. My stack of mail was two feet high. I felt instantaneously overwhelmed, and I would sit at my desk for hours looking out the window at the mountains. I was having trouble concentrating on anything save my desire to lace up my boots and dive headlong back into the woods, where life is not only much simpler, but much more rewarding and compelling.

The pace of life off the trail astounded me. The first time I got behind the wheel of my truck after returning home, I was cruising merrily down the highway at about 30 miles per hour, thinking how strange it was to be able to knock off two days' worth of hiking in a single hour. Behind me, vehicles were honking their horns and flashing their lights and making obscene gestures and calling me names as they passed. I tried to drive faster, but the increase in speed was too much to handle after spending nine weeks and 740 miles strolling along at 2 mph, which is a very sane pace. Several weeks passed before I could make myself drive 55, and, when it finally happened, I felt like I'd just broken the sound barrier.

There have been numerous magazine articles penned on the subject of post-long-hike decompression, which usually lasts at least as long as the time you were gone. It's a near-overwhelming, near-debilitating combination of a hangover and jet lag. You walk around day after day disoriented and lethargic, and, if you're not careful, you can really start to drift and lose momentum during this time. You have to work hard to regain your focus on life in the context of civilization, which can make you feel sick to your stomach just thinking about it.

Then, you get to the point where you have been back longer than you were gone, and, suddenly, you start looking at your long, intense and wonderful hike as a memory rather than a work in progress. You start to regain some of the weight you lost while tromping through the mountains, and you notice that your friends are starting to weary of your trail stories.

For four months after leaving the CDT, I dreamed almost nightly about backpacking. Throughout the winter of 1996–97, I donned my snowshoes or skis and hit the woods with Cali almost daily — often at the expense of work. I overheard Gay tell a friend of mine at one point that it was obvious all I thought about now was being alone with my dog in the hills.

By the time spring-like weather finally started arriving in the High Country, I was just starting to get a grip on the post-CDT John Fayhee personality. To say I had been worried about who I now was and where I was going is an understatement. While I was on the Appalachian Trail, I had decided that, come hell or high water, I was going to get serious about being a writer. After I left the AT, I beelined my way back to college and, within six months, I was getting paid to churn out words.

While hiking the Colorado Trail, I had decided to pursue martial arts training and, within four years, I was a black belt in Tae Kwon Do.

Try though I might on the CDT, I could not come up with any goals like those -— goals that not only are palpable but that necessitate some degree of positive personality transformation by their very pursuit.

Then, it dawned on me: Though I may not have left the CDT with any sort of specific lifestyle goal, I came away from the trail with a new understanding of my life. After spending a long winter snowshoeing and skiing through the majestic Summit County backcountry, it slowly began to sink in that, by my very actions, I was demonstrating a new and hopefully better personality model. I no longer was interested in spending my free time hanging out in bars or socializing just for the sake of keeping company with my fellow human beings. I had become what I think I knew I was all along — a card-carrying woods person. I suddenly understood that the direction of my life had been determined, and the CDT helped bring that understanding into focus. Heretofore, I had always intellectually looked upon long trips into the wilderness as diversions from life, and the process of writing about those experiences as a good enough way to make a living until I started pursuing more serious subjects. I had said many times over the years that, if I was still writing about backpacking trips when I was 50, I would be sorely disappointed in myself.

The CDT taught me that there is no higher calling than taking long hikes and penning tomes about those hikes, and, for that realization, I will always be indebted to that trail and my time upon it.

A large part of this self-understanding process no doubt came about because of the essential nature of the CDT — the fact that it is ultra-challenging on all fronts. Looking back, I don't know if my experience and the lifestyle/personality conclusions I drew from my experience could have come about had the CDT not been gnarly in the extreme. In retrospect, there are a few places — mainly those that follow unappealing dirt roads — that I would like to see improved. And I wouldn't mind seeing a few more trail signs. But, all in all, I hope fervently that the CDT maintains its exclusive, ultra-demanding character. But I'm afraid the CDT in 20 years will be much different from the CDT of today. I am concerned that it will be too well marked and mapped. I am afraid that it will become hopelessly influenced by and molded in the image of the very forces of civilization that people need desperately to escape as often as possible.

I want other people who have been as badly polluted by civilization as I was that long-ago day, wondering where the hell the trail was on Cumbres Pass, to have the opportunity to cinch up their pack and head out onto the CDT, where tranquility, insight and rewarding physical exertion in the extreme await like a soothing psychological salve.

Along Colorado's Continental Divide Trail